25

THINGS

YOU CAN DO TO

FEEL

BETTER

RIGHT

NOW!

Bill Chandler

Andante Publishing
Redmond, Washington

Cover photo by Gordon Macdonald

Andante Publishing
Post Office Box 507
Redmond, Washington 98073-0507

Table Of Contents

Dedication

To my family, my never-ending source of inspiration and joy.

Acknowledgement

I would like to thank my friends —
known and unknown — who make my
dreams possible, and ever so much more
fun.

"What is, is best."
Buddha

Introduction

verything we do is in an effort to make us feel better. No exceptions. This may seem like a trivial self-centered thing to spend our precious lifetime doing but in actuality, it is our one and only purpose for being here. All religion, all psychology, and all theology is directed toward helping us in this endeavor, and the only reason we participate in these disciplines is in an effort to feel better. There are no exceptions.

Why is it so difficult to feel better about ourselves every single waking moment? Because we are playing a spiritual game on a physical plane. We have become accustomed to using our sensory devices to define for us what is real and what is not real. It is like trying to use a map of the stars to guide you through the streets of New York City. It isn't going to work. You cannot get to where you want to go no matter how hard you try. It will make no sense, and it will be a frustrating journey. But, if you put a New York

City street map in your hand, the journey becomes a piece of cake.

We are on a treasure hunt, and we are blindfolded. Actually, we are worse than blindfolded. We are being given misinformation. Our challenge is to put the seemingly real misinformation aside and listen for clues that will guide us to the treasure. The treasure is our self. We must find our self at all cost. Fortunately we are given clues all along the way. The most accurate guidance system we have is the way we feel. If we will simply follow our feelings we will proceed on the most straightforward path directly to the treasure.

There are two types of things you can do that will make you feel better right now. There are the temporary illusion-creating fantasies, and there are those that make you feel better because you are taking a step toward the divine design of your life.

Most of us seek to attain our peace through the artificial state — the illusion-creating fantasy. We flaunt our wealth, our car, our home, our body, our position, our religion, our children, and numerous other facades in an effort to help us feel better. Some of us even choose to snort cocaine, down a shot of whiskey, drive fast, go to sleep, or have addictive sex. The reason we do these things is because they work. They can definitely make us feel better right now, but they are like borrowing money at the bank. It feels good now, but you're going to be paying for it for a long, long time.

This book is about the other methods, the steps you can take that will invite serenity into your world and lead you ever closer to the divine design of your individual life. As you take these steps you will begin to know the truth about yourself, and the truth will indeed make you free.

You will then know with certainty that there is no end to the degree of goodness you can feel about yourself and the world around you. There is no point of "arriving" at total goodness or nirvana or heaven. There is only you as a child of the Universe doing the best you know how to walk toward the light.

My hope is that the ideas presented in this book will help you to know exactly what to do to invite harmony into your life so that you may unload burdens, know truth, take action, express love, and walk in greater peace today. This is what every human being is seeking. It is the goal of the divine within us. It is the purpose of life. In the words of a master, "Man is that he might have joy." Sounds great to me!

*"No man is an island,
No man stands alone ... "*

1

The Lonely Fiddle

"Ask for help? Me? Why in the world would I ask for help? I mean, what would I ask for? I'm pretty self-sufficient you know. I don't really need anything from anybody, at least nothing I can think of."

Sounds familiar doesn't it? I know it hits a chord with me. The internal dialogue that goes along with this attitude sounds something like this:

"I don't need anyone. Oh yeah, I like getting Christmas cards and everything, but if everyone else in the world disappeared I'd be all right. I might have trouble cutting my hair and stuff like that but I'd figure something out."

What this person is really saying is "I am scared to death. I feel totally inadequate, and I don't want anyone to know it. If I admitted I need someone else that would mean that I am in some way incomplete and it's bad enough being incomplete, but if anyone else knew I was incomplete that would be awful. What would everyone think? If I asked for help they would all know."

We run around in our isolated illusions trying to pretend we are the whole thing when the truth is that we are only a part of the whole thing — a small and vital part, but only one part none the less. We act like a piston pretending to be a car, a telephone that thinks it's the phone company, or a violin that believes it's the entire symphony orchestra. We have somehow gotten it into our head that if we are not the whole thing we are inadequate. Breathe a great big sigh of relief. You are not the whole thing, you are not supposed to be the whole thing, and you never were supposed to be the whole thing. That's why God put a whole bunch of us on the same planet. Isn't that great to know? Now you can dump the 500 pound rugged individualist attitude you've been carrying around for the past 30 years. The best news is that our lives will function more smoothly and peacefully by doing less if we will only focus on doing our own infinitesimal part the very best we know how and call on others when we need help.

I once planned to spend the day getting our house ready to sell because we were going to show it at noon the following day. Before I got started, a friend who was facing some challenges called and we talked for a while. As soon as we finished talking I had to run to the store to get some supplies for a meeting that night. When I returned home, an old client called to tell me how well his invention was selling. While I was still on the phone my wife interrupted to see if I would run downtown and help a friend of ours who couldn't get her car started.

After helping our friend I had a late lunch which

was interrupted by a herd of cattle running all over our lawn. This was getting to be too much. I saddled up my steed and spent the next hour helping the buckaroo get his beef back where it was supposed to be. I then gave two of my insistent children a "Horsey ride." By the time I put my mount away it was time to do the neighborhood cub scout run as my wife was busy going to our daughter's ballet recital. The cub scout run took an hour longer than expected because Robert wasn't sure which Aunt's house I was supposed to drop him off at. As it ends up, none of his Aunts were home, but that was okay because it was the wrong day anyway. By the time I got him home, his mother was frantic thinking I'd absconded with her son. When I finally arrived home everyone else had already eaten dinner and I was the bad guy because I got home late again. Thank God it was dark, because I was too bushed to mow the lawn as I had said I would, and thank God my wife doesn't know the lawn mower has headlights.

The next morning the alarm went off at five o'clock and I mumbled,

"How in the world am I going to get the house ready to show by noon?"

"Maybe Loren would come over and give you a hand" was my wife Lori's response.

I lay in bed and agonized for another hour until the sun was coming up.

"Maybe you should call Loren."

"Why should I call Loren?"

"How is he going to know you need help if you don't call him and ask him?" 7:00 a.m., I prop myself up on the side of the bed. I look at the phone and realize that Lori had asked a very appropriate question. "Why don't I call Loren?" He is a good friend who would do anything for me. He lives close-by, he works his own schedule, and I've done things to help him (as if that matters). I know he'd be glad to help, but for some reason I resist calling.

My brain is now functioning enough for a little introspection and I realize that I believe there is something wrong with asking for help, as if I were irresponsible or I had screwed up or something. I pick up the phone despite protests from my ego. I call Loren. He zaps over, we have a blast whipping the place into shape by eleven o'clock, and we both feel great. What's the big deal? The big deal is that I've got this demented individualist syndrome. I spend all day responding to other's requests, but I am too proud to reveal my own needs. I fix cars, call friends, bus kids, run errands, give free consulting and help misguided bucka-roos, but I have an awfully hard time asking for what I need. I used to have trouble asking the man at the gas sta-tion to pump my gas, and this was before they had self-serve gas stations. What a shame. I'm getting over it though and finding some interesting side effects: I appre-ciate people more, I feel better, I have more friends, I get a whole lot more done, and I am more at peace.

To ask for help is to admit your humanness. To say "I am an imperfect growing child of the Universe trying to make my way through this ole' world and I need some help right now" — what could be more honest? What could make you more real, more sincere, more approach-able, more divine? This is the kind of person we all want to be with, why do we find it so difficult to be one?

When you ask for help you find that your physical burdens disappear because you have help with them. Your emotional burdens disappear because you are revealing your real self, and your relationships improve because it's hard not to love people who are true to themselves.

This doesn't mean you should start thinking up things you can get other people to do for you that you could do for yourself. We all know how old that gets. It simply means to do the best you can. Walk calmly through life helping others when they need it and asking for help when you need it. If we could all follow this simple counsel for one week we would literally find heaven on earth. Wouldn't that feel great? The violin alone makes a miserable symphony, but when he calls on his friends the music is sublime.

"The choice is always safety or freedom —
I choose freedom."

2

Do It Different

*"If you always do what you've always done,
You'll always get what you've always got."*

S ix o'clock in the morning, the alarm goes off. Six-
fifteen, crawl out of bed. Six-twenty shower,
dress, complain about the weather, left shoe, right
shoe, red tie, wake up the kids, coffee, toast, dread
the day, kiss the wife, look at watch, kiss the kids, start car,
back out, first left, second right, accelerate to 50, seven
miles, slow down, right at light, into lot, third spot on left,
look at watch, grab case, shut door, key in left pocket, look
at watch, cross street, open door, up stairs, "Hi Mary,"
down hall, third door on right, pickup list, sit in chair, look
at watch, read list . . .

You're now two hours into your day and you
haven't used your mind yet. It can be quite efficient to do
life that way, but it isn't a whole lot of fun. It's an emotion-

less way to live, yet it is the path the mortal part of us seeks. A path of conformity that can, on occasion, lead to great accomplishment, but the accomplishments are moot because they are not yours. They have nothing to do with you, they have only to do with what other people think, and what other people think doesn't matter — at all.

Computers can do "efficient," but that isn't life, that is existence. Computers exist, people live, at least some of them do. The rest of us spend our allotted time in a no-man's-land somewhere between life and existence. It goes something like this: "I want to live a rich, full life; I want to become all I am here to become; I want to make my dreams come true; — but, I don't know how to do that stuff. Besides, it sounds sort of scary. I'm not that much of a risk taker so I'll just have my sub-conscious look back into my ancestral files to find out how it was done in the past. Then I'll know the "right way," and I'll be happy like they were.

The problem is that, #1) "They" probably weren't happy in the first place, so you are using a model for unhappiness in an attempt to be happy, and #2) even if they were happy, your diet for happiness is yours and yours alone. So, it is impossible to get "there" by following another's plan. In the words of William Blake, "One law for the lion and ox is oppression."

Doing things a little differently shakes up your psyche. Your psyche is using the composite knowledge of the ages to help you operate in as safe a way as possible — no matter how miserable it makes you. To do things differently is to send yourself a powerful new message. You are telling yourself that there is something more important than safety — I call it life. In a very real sense, you give up your life every time you let your psyche play it safe. The road to your joy will not be a safe one. This does not mean to drive recklessly or stop wearing your seat belt; it simply means that if you are going to get to your place of peace, you are going to have to take risks.

Some of you are undoubtedly saying, "Why, I take risks all the time. I invested millions in onions when everyone told me not to, and I go bungy jumping every Thursday morning." Yes, those are risks, but they are nothing compared to telling your wayward son you love him, apologizing to your wife, or weeping before an audience. The real risks are invisible. They require you to put your ego on the crap table and roll the dice.

Hard? Of course it's hard. It's hard because it appears to be you that's up for grabs. Relax, it's not you, it's just your ego. The problem is that you think you are your ego. Yet once you become its master, the real you begins to shine forth. The good news is that God is the croupier and he's going to give you every seven. So all you've got to do is stay in the game and keep on rolling the dice. It might look bad for a while, but isn't it nice to know that you can't lose if you keep on playing the game?

Chances are that unless you have put some conscious effort into raising your consciousness, you are still operating on ancestral autopilot. You are unconsciously living the life your ancestors have led for millennia untold. The props are different, but the script is the same. You may attain a degree of "Pseudo-joy" when you come close to "Doing it right," but you will never know the "Peace that surpasseth all understanding." This can only come from living the life you are here to live, unencumbered by the plague of shoulds and oughts from ages gone by.

When in this state of awareness or higher consciousness we may still do many of the same things and go many of the same places, but our experience will be entirely different. Life becomes an amusing adventure rather than drudgery. You will take nothing seriously, including yourself, and you will see the comical in almost every moment. The best part is that it will be virtually impossible for anyone or anything to bother you. You may be attacked, insulted, and dragged through the mud, but you will recognize the actions as your attacker's problem, not yours. You will spend each moment wondering what the next magical moment will bring to your experience.

This is such a joyous way to live compared to living on ancestral autopilot. Unfortunately, most of us spend our entire life on ancestral autopilot; acting out a predetermined role that allows us to maintain mortal consciousness at the least possible risk. This involves doing everything the way it has always been done because it is the "Right" way. The problem with autopilot is that it does not allow us to live. I mean that very literally. Life consists of a series of experiences which allow us to learn by trial and error how to provide ourselves with the greatest degree of freedom. Autopilot is the path of avoiding these experiences and denying ourselves the joy and freedom of self-mastery. I don't know how God feels, but I would feel like I wasted my money if I sent my kid to Disneyland and he didn't go on any of the rides. My question to my child would be, "Why on earth did you want to go to Disneyland in the first place?"

I was once washing my windshield at a self-service gas station in Yakima, Washington. I was about to drop the squeegee thing back into the bucket when I noticed an older woman waiting in the passenger seat of a car on the other side of the pump. For some reason I went over and washed her windshield too, then I ran in, paid, smiled at her, and drove away. She didn't smile, she never said anything, she just stared at me like I was the strangest thing she had ever seen. I got a kick out of it. I laughed all the way home. I still think about it whenever I go to that gas station. I did something a little bit differently, and I was well rewarded. I imagine she probably doesn't get gas there anymore because the people are weird.

We take our patterns so seriously, even when they are not of our own making. Especially if we think they are pleasing to God, to our parents, to the IRS, or to whichever structure we live in fear of. Little do we know that the purpose of our life is to learn to be true to ourself — at all cost. If only we understood that there is really only one universal commandment: "Be Happy." That is all we are here to do, and we have everything we need to do it inside of us. The only reason we listen to counsel from others is because we don't trust ourselves, yet trusting yourself is the only way to get where you want to be.

You may appear to be a free roving spirit to others if your rut happens to involve fame or fortune or a particular type of prestige, but in your heart you are still a donkey chained to the kiddy ride. 'Round and 'round you go, doing exactly what you are told to do, digging your rut ever deeper, trying to convince yourself that this is what you chose to do, and justifying your own fears by condemning others. We become so distraught when one of our playmates dies, yet we think nothing of throwing our own life away a little bit at a time. That is what we do with every minute we spend not fully alive. Every moment we spend acting out our predetermined program without being aware of our existence and of all the choices available to us is a moment wasted.

Exactly how do you do this "Break out of your rut" stuff? It's easy, and it's a lot of fun. All you have to do is start doing things in different ways than you usually do them. It's easiest to start with little things. Sleep on the other side of the bed, tie your right shoe first, get to work five minutes early, put the forks in the dishwasher upside down; everything you do can be done a different way. If you're adventuresome you might try dumping a pile of laundry on the floor when your mother-in-law is coming over, or not paying one of your bills for a few months. It doesn't matter what or how you change, it only matters that you start doing at least some of the simplest things you do differently. Here are a few simple ideas to get you started:

- Wear your watch on the other wrist
- Drive home from work the long way
- Cut your hair differently
- Bring your wife flowers for no reason at all
- Don't yell at your kids for a whole day — no matter what
- Get up early and watch the sun rise
- Dress weird
- Wash your car
- Let your car get dirty
- Say No
- Say Yes
- Wear socks that don't match
- Don't wear a tie
- Wear a tie
- Don't talk for a whole day
- Stay in bed all day and take it easy
- Stay up all night

You may find that your old way works best; that's okay, the purpose in doing this is not to develop new unconscious habits that are more efficient than your old ones. The purpose is to shake up your psyche. You may not be strong enough to break out of your rut in one fell swoop. That's okay too — you don't have to. You weaken the walls and then break them down one little brick at a time, simply by changing your patterns. Every time you make a change you are taking one small step toward freeing your true self, and every step you take will make you feel better because you are reclaiming the conscious power within you. The power that can indeed move mountains, and calm the seas; but remember, the masters who do those kinds of things didn't happen out into the country one Sunday afternoon and decide that Kilamanjaro was in the wrong place. They began as unconscious beings just like you and I. Then one day they decided to walk home a different way, and thus their journey began.

"What you fear does not exist."

3

Take Action Anyway

"*I*t's impossible, you just can't get there from here." Take action anyway.

"It's never been done before and I don't think it ever will be." Take action anyway.

"My wife would have a fit, and my parents would think I was crazy." Take action anyway.

"If it doesn't work I'll look like a fool." Take action anyway.

"I just can't figure out what to do." Take action anyway.

"People will think I'm stuck-up or something." Take action anyway!

It doesn't matter what other people think. It doesn't matter if no one has ever done it that way before. It doesn't matter what statistics say. It doesn't matter if your idea is crazy. It doesn't even matter if it works or not. The only thing that matters is that you take action in the direction in which you want to go.

There is always something we want — why don't we go for it? Why would we not take action toward something we want? Fear, and fear alone. Fear that the process might be painful, and fear that the result we want would be painful. Fear of the process warns "Yes, I would like to be on the other side of the forest, but it might be scary, and I might get hurt, and I might get lost, and I might not make it, and people might laugh at me, and there are probably zillions of other things that will happen to me that I don't even know about. No thank you. I'd rather stay right here where it's safe than take a chance like that."

Fear of the end result sounds like this: "Oh yea, I'm pretty sure I can make it, and I'm not too afraid of those things in the forest, but I'm not sure I would like it over there. I mean nobody in my family has ever been over there. They might think I'm crazy. They might even disown me — you never know. And I'm not sure I would be able to handle that kind of life anyway. Don't get me wrong, I'd like it and everything, I'm just afraid that I'd probably start drinking again, or chasing women, or getting into some sort of trouble. Besides, all my friends live on this side of the forest and it might be lonely over there."

Where does this fear come from? It comes from our experiences of the past. It is our extrapolation of pain we have experienced in the past — probably before we were three years old. Like the elephant who is held fast with a piece of string, or the horse that won't go near a strand of uncharged electric fence. It is our beliefs that are keeping us captive, not reality. Rather than do our best to succeed, so many of us choose to guarantee our demise by not even trying.

The good news is that there will probably be no

pain as there was in the past. Even if there is, it is worth experiencing it and getting on with our existence. You might as well get it over with anyway because the place you are sitting is going to become more and more painful until it exceeds the pain of that you fear. This is nature's way of getting you to take action. Irene Cara says it all in the opening lines of *Flashdance,*

"First when there's nothing, but a slow growing dream,
That your fear seems to hide, deep inside your mind.
All alone I have cried, silent tears full of pride,
In a world made of steel, made of stone."

While it is imperative for us to take action, it is also imperative that we take appropriate action. Cutting down a tree in the forest with an axe seems like a fairly easy task. We just go out into the forest, pick a tree, and start swinging. No matter how weak we are, how dull our axe is, how big the tree is, or how bad a shot we are — the tree will eventually fall. So it is with the challenges of our life. Unfortunately most of us sharpen our axe and exercise, but when we get out into the forest we start running around from tree to tree, chopping here and there, and wondering why the trees aren't falling down around us. But the three-year-old sits down by a big oak with a kitchen knife, and before we know it we hear him yell "Timber." The incredible power of appropriate action.

Now I'll tell you about my challenge. My challenge is to relax, to let go, to take appropriate action when the appropriate action is to do nothing. I can't stand it. I have a hard time believing that anything will happen if I don't do it myself. This sounds like a noble take-responsibility type of attitude, but it doesn't allow for grace or serendipity or a helping hand from our fellow travelers, yet these are the things that are really going to get us where we want to go.

While attending college I worked as a dorm manager for a couple of years. One Friday night we were having an all-campus dance in our dorm. I stopped by my room for a few minutes and while there I had another visit from my forlorn friend I'll call Tom. Tom was having girl problems again. "Willy," he said, "How am I ever going to get a girlfriend?" He then proceeded to tell my how awful he felt, and how he just didn't think there were any girls that would ever like him. I consoled him for a while and then he explained that he had been in his room praying for hours and hours and that once again God had not answered his prayers.

"There are hundreds of single girls right downstairs and they're all looking for a guy" I explained. "Maybe God brought her all the way across campus for you, thinking you could handle the trip downstairs. I mean what kind of girl would walk up to the third floor of a men's dorm and knock on the door of a guy's room she didn't even know?"

"Gee, I never thought of that, that could be it, couldn't it?"

"Could be."

"Thanks Willy, I never thought of it that way." He raced downstairs to see what God had delivered, and sure enough a few days later he had staked his inseparable claim.

Now I don't think things work quite like Tom believes, but I do know that serendipity requires action. Serendipity is defined as "the faculty of finding valuable or agreeable things not sought for." Some people call it luck, I call it serendipity. Big difference. Luck is thought to be something fortunate happening without a cause. An effect without a cause. Impossible, there is no such thing, never has been, never will be. Just because the cause-effect relationship exists in the unseen world doesn't mean it doesn't exist; however, your actions are not directly connected to the results. I had a hard time getting this, but once it became clear, life made a lot more sense.

How does taking action work? On the surface it seems as if it is the action itself that is getting you from here to there, but it is not. It is the change in your beliefs. At first this sounds absurd, especially if you are one who is rigidly attached to the expression of your ego. The truth is that while it is the action of putting one leg in front of the other that transported your body through the deep dark forest, it was your mind that was doing the directing, and it was the mastery of your illusory mortal fears that allowed you to go to a new place where you hadn't been before. So action works in three ways:

1) Taking action brings you closer to your nemesis so that you can see more clearly that it is not as nemesizing as you had originally believed.

2) Taking action presents a clear concise message to your inner being and to all the other cosmic forces of the Universe that let the powers waiting to assist you know the direction in which you want to go.

3) Finally, after you have faced the fears of Step #1, and sent the message of Step #2, then, and only then can physical action take you from where you are to where you want to be.

In our limited mortal thinking we like to plan out exactly what is going to happen, and then proceed to follow our imaginary Yellow Brick Road. It doesn't work that way. Yes, you might eventually get to your desired goal, but I can assure you that you didn't get there exactly as you had planned. I think it's wonderful, but some people get all upset when they deviate from their plan, as if they are supposed to be some divine oracle that can foresee the future. That is not our responsibility, or our objective. Our only sensible goal is to define where we want to go and start walking in that direction.

In High School I was in a play which stopped midstream, on opening night, with the good fairies on the stage about to begin their dance. The pause was long and uncomfortable. The fairies looked at one another wondering what to do, the rest of us were getting embarrassed. Finally our teacher got up and walked behind the curtain to see what the problem was. He found that the fairies were waiting for the musicians to start playing and the musicians were waiting for the fairies to start dancing. If only someone had taken action.

Flashdance closes with these words:

"What a feeling, being's believin',
I can have it all now I'm dancing for my life.
Take your passion, and make it happen.
Pictures come alive, now I'm dancing through my life."

Whatever your dream, wherever you are, whatever you have or haven't done in the past, now is the time to take action. Focus clearly on the life of your fondest dream and start dancing, knowing, that the moment you start to dance the music will begin to play.

4

Call Me By Name

I know it sounds absurd to think that you will feel better if you call other people by name, but it's true. In order to actualize this you have to go back to the original postulate that the degree to which we feel good about ourselves is the degree to which we attempt to make others feel good. Therefore, anything we do that makes others feel good will make us feel good by default. How was that for a major and a minor premise?

What does this have to do with calling people by name? As you probably already know, people like to hear their name. This doesn't mean that I jump for joy when my wife says "Bill, bill, bill, bill" as she flips through the mail. It means that people like to be addressed by their name. Why do people like to be addressed by name? Because, by just using their name you are making a statement that you care enough about them to have allocated a portion of your cerebral cortex to information about them.

You are saying that they are important to you. It may not seem like much, but we remember what is important to us. Do you remember the name of your first love, your best friend, or your elementary school teacher? It may have been a while, but their names are probably easily accessible because they are important to you.

If you don't think this name-calling business is important, try this experiment. The next time you're out on a date with Lucy, call her Mary two or three times. Chances are you won't even get up to bat. Or, if you're married to Penelope, pretend you're asleep and talk about Betty Lou in an affectionate way. I bet your breakfast won't be waiting for you in the morning.

It's a funny thing, but knowing a person's name is the first step in caring, and calling a person by name is one small way of expressing your love for them. As with all expressions of love, there is risk involved in calling a person by name. Small as it may seem, there is the fear that they may wonder why you've bothered to remember their name. They may become suspicious. Worse yet, you may call them the wrong name. It is much safer not to call people by name. You won't make an embarrassing mistake, you won't have to let them know you care, and you won't be criticized, but you also won't reap the self-enhancing reward of taking the risk of expressing love to another human being.

The worst thing you can do is not call a person by name because you're afraid you might goof up. Give it a shot anyway. If you guess wrong they will correct you and you'll probably remember it in the future. The very worst thing you can do is to not figure out a person's name until your wives end up being best friends and you get put in the embarrassing position of having to introduce your nameless cohort to the group. He who thought you were a blood brother now thinks you don't care, and you lose.

How many times have you been at one of those social things where you are introduced to a circle of people whose names you couldn't recall 30 seconds later? Numerous times I suspect. Here's a trick that works well for me. First you have to forget about what kind of impression you are making. If you are thinking about that kind of ego stuff you will never get there. The next step is to focus on each person's eyes as you are introduced, and say their name several times in your head. Then notice something that stands out about them. Not something about their clothes like blue suit or red dress, because they may be on their way up to slip into something more comfortable. Try something significant about them, and try to make it positive. It can be a physical characteristic: nice voice, red hair, no hair, green eyes, beautiful; or a personality trait: likes boats, obnoxious, spiritual, extremely shy. The stranger it is the better. So while everybody else is frantically contemplating the impressions they are making, you are looking your newfound friends in the eye and saying to yourself something like this:

"Jenny, Jenny, Jenny — Beautiful;
Rob, Rob, Rob — Nice voice;
Sam, Sam, Sam — Character;
Ian, Ian, Ian — English accent;
Sue, Sue, Sue — Red hair."

Then, if you really want to be effective, and if your master of ceremonies is slow, you can add a review of each person's name. It goes like this:

"Jenny, Jenny, Jenny — Beautiful;
Rob, Rob, Rob — Nice voice — Jenny, Rob;
Sam, Sam, Sam — Character — Jenny, Rob, Sam ;

Ian, Ian, Ian — English accent — Jenny Rob, Sam, Ian;

Sue, Sue, Sue — Red hair — Jenny, Rob, Sam, Ian, Sue."

Be sure to look each person in the eye as you think their name. This may sound like cheating — but it's not — you are putting effort into them. You are bringing them into your consciousness in a greater way. You are allocating a greater portion of your cerebral cortex to them. You are taking one minute step on the path of becoming one, and they will appreciate it.

While I was going to college I had a video games route where I supplied video games, pool tables, juke boxes, and pinball games to various businesses. When I started I had nine competitors. When I sold it I had none. They had all gone out of business or had sold their business to me. I thought I was a pretty good businessman until I was asked point blank how I did it. My immediate response was almost something about running a tight ship or being a good manager. But I realized that none of those things were true. When it really came down to it, there was only one thing I did better than all of my competitors. My red book. I had a red two ring binder with a 5 x 8 card in it for each account. On each card was written the name of the account, the owner, the owner's spouse, the employees' names, and anything else I knew about them. I might finish collecting from the Time Out Tavern and write down, "Run by Ron Smith, owned by his mother Matilda, Matilda is at home sick with pneumonia, Ron rides a Harley."

Then, the next time I go up there, I open my book, review the last entry, and I go in to find Matilda behind the bar. "Hi Matilda, looks like you're feeling a lot better." She is surprised that I know so much about her and goes on to tell me about how awful she felt and how much better she feels now. When I leave we both feel a little better about ourselves. Then I move on to BJ's Bar and Grill. "Hi Renee, how was your trip to Montana?"

My conversations with these people became deeper and deeper until we found ourselves sharing our dreams, our hopes, and our fears. It all began by calling them by name.

Then a funny thing happened. I was cleaning out my car one spring day when I found my red book under the seat. I dusted it off, flipped through the pages, and found that my last entry was over six months ago — yet I hadn't missed a beat. The effort I put into getting to know these people had resulted in really knowing them — in caring, in wishing them well, in friendships and support and all the other socially acceptable names we have for love. I later sold the business and, with a few exceptions, those who were once ready to bite my head off because I wouldn't increase their take by 5 percent were now wishing me well. The serendipitous part of the whole thing is that the friendships I gained will last far longer than the cash flow. It is also interesting to note that my feeble expressions of love came before the cash flow. It would never have worked the other way.

Even though I used my book which seemed a little like cheating, I was putting effort into these people and they responded; but it wasn't their response that made me feel better, it was the miniscule expressions of love I offered. My initial plan was not to gain new accounts, but to be on good terms with the people. It is amazing to see that even in business, love is the answer.

"Your life is the composite of your thoughts."

5

Commit To Commit

C ommit to commit? Why on earth would I want to do that? Making a commitment means agreeing now to do something I may later not want to do, or to not do something I may later want to do. When later comes, I may not want to keep my commitment and then I'll either not keep it and feel guilty, or else I'll keep it so I don't feel guilty, but then I'll feel bad because I didn't really want to keep it. It's a whole lot easier for me if I just don't make commitments.

It is true that it is a lot easier not to make commitments, but remember where the easy road goes — down, down, down. "I'm not going to make a commitment" says the alcoholic. "I can control my drinking. The next time I'm out at 'The Keg' with the boys feeling depressed I'll just pass, I'll have a glass of water, you watch." Unfortunately most of us have watched — time and time again.

The need for commitment is obvious — the man at the bar, the girl in the back seat, the overweight housewife, the cocaine addict, the workaholic husband — the list goes on and on. But what about the more subtle deviants? Those who struggle with commitments of omission. The boy who yearns to play the piano but doesn't practice, the future basketball star who does all of his practicing in his head, the woman who is going to go back to school — someday. I believe that more harm is done by those who don't commit to their dream each day than by those who won't stop their vice in a lifetime. Not only that, but if those with an overpowering vice would commit to their dream, their vice would begin to fade into oblivion. That is the way the universe works.

You cannot rid yourself of something you are focused on; so the trick to eliminating your vice is to change your focus. The problem is that we become habitually, physically and psychically dependent upon our vice and it holds us fast in it's iron jaws. I think that's why they call it a "vice." Freedom comes through changing our focus. There is only one power strong enough to bring about this change. A power that's been at our beck and call since the day we were born. It is the power of commitment — a sincere commitment to be true to ourselves. When we deny ourselves, we are held in bondage. It is only through this commitment that we can ever summon the universal energy necessary to become free. Our freedom is the only thing we want badly enough to take the risks and experience the pain of self-actualization for. But experience it we must or stagnation sets in and we begin to slip down, down, down into a self-created isolation commonly known as hell. And believe me, you don't have to die to get there.

How many of us are carrying burdens that consist

of keeping commitments we didn't make in the first place? How many of us are leading a life of torment because we are trying to live our own life, and at the same time keep commitments we never made? Sounds absurd but it is going on all the time. If you didn't make the commitment, dump it.

In my later teens I was told by some well-meaning clergy that when I was baptized as a child I had made a commitment to God that I would be a missionary. After grilling these poor men about what that means they told me that it means to do whatever your church leaders tell you, and we are your church leaders who have been ordained by God to guide you at this time in your life. No wonder I don't like commitments. I left that meeting saying, "Who do those guys think they are, telling me what commitments I've made? I don't remember making those commitments, and besides, even if I did, it was some kind of trick." Absurd as it may seem, I wasted far too many of my precious moments struggling with the actualization of a commitment that I didn't make. I may not be able to get those moments back, but you can be sure I won't be wasting any more of my allotted time living up to commitments someone else is making for me.

Then there are those of us who are throttled by commitments we made in the past that no longer serve us. If you made a commitment that no longer serves your long-term best interest, drop it like a hot potato. This doesn't mean to dump your wife because she burned the chow, or to ditch your husband because the trash is piled sky high. It means that when you are totally clear about a commitment from the past, and it is in your own best interest to decommit, then by all means do so. If it is a significant commitment, it may take a year or two for clarity to come. Be careful, if ever haste made waste, this is the place.

I once committed to my mother that I wouldn't drive in the street anymore. A wise thing to do at the time considering: I was 10 years old, I had just been hauled home by the police, and I was going to lose my brakeless homemade motorized go-cart if I didn't. Obviously, keeping the commitment to stop driving in the street no longer serves my personal long-term best interest, yet it kept me alive, "in wheels," and out of jail at the time.

"But commitments are so hard" I hear you say. I agree, they can be, but that's like saying "every time I hit myself it hurts." Stop hitting yourself so hard. You are the one making the commitments so don't make them so hard. We expect ourselves to be superhuman, and we beat ourselves up when we aren't. Did Mr. America bench press three hundred pounds his first time? No way. He probably started with fifty. He did fifty lbs. over and over until it was easy and then he moved on to sixty. We don't allow ourselves that leisure. We want to go from zero to sixty — NOW.

I used to make New Years resolutions that, like the rest of the world's, rarely lasted a week. The list usually looked something like this except it was much longer:
- Get up at five o'clock every morning
- Exercise for one hour every morning
- Spend thirty minutes in silent meditation every day
- Spend fifteen minutes alone with each child every day
- Write for two hours every day
- Take my wife out every week
- Eat three meals every day
- Always be on time

• Etc. etc. etc.

Every New Year's Day I would look back on the previous year's resolutions and copy them down for the next year. It was absurd. Finally I fessed up to my humanness, and my commitments changed significantly. They also hurt a lot less to make, and for once, I kept them. My new list looks something like this:

• Get up every day
• Practice the piano five minutes each day
• Write in my journal once a week
• Spend at least one minute alone with each family member daily
• Write for at least fifteen minutes five days a week
• Spend five minutes in quiet contemplation each day
• Read something I enjoy for one minute each day.
• Do 36 push-ups every week-day

It's easy now, I even like doing it. I like reading and writing and playing the piano. I like spending time with my wife and kids. I even like writing in my journal. The only part that bugs me is when I do one of my late night creative marathons and arrive at my bedside at four o'clock a.m. without having done my push-ups, I'm pooped, but I drop to my knees as my wife pulls the pillow over her head. 1 - 2 - 3 . . . They may be the wimpiest push-ups you've ever seen . . . 14 - 15 - 16 . . . but I do them anyway because, I'm committed! . . . 25 - 26 - 27 . . . but you couldn't see them anyway because . . . 31 - 32 - 33 . . . it's dark . . . 36 . . . because I'd die if anyone saw me doing wimpy push-ups in my underwear in the middle of the night.

Albert Gray tells us that the universal secret of success is that "Successful people do the things that failures don't like to do." How do we start doing these success sowing things? We commit, and the forthcoming power helps us make short-term decisions that will help us reach our long-term goals.

The secret of getting commitments to work for you is to begin by making simple commitments. I will not drink on Sunday; I will not eat fudge before noon; I will spend three minutes focused solely on my son when he gets home from school each day; I will not complain about my spouse in front of other people; I will do two push-ups every other day — little tiny baby steps toward the You you want to be.

When you keep your commitments not only do you become more adept at whatever it is you have committed to do, you also begin to develop a feeling of internal power, confidence, and self control. Each time you make a decision that is in your own best interest, no matter how insignificant it may seem, you are sending yourself a powerful new message. You are beginning to recognize your word as universal law instead of moot sound waves. You are voting for yourself, you are sending a message to the universe that you are capable of controlling the unlimited power available to man. And sure enough, as soon as man is capable of controlling power, he begins to realize how much of it the universe has already placed at his beck and call.

The rungs on the ladder of spiritual growth are commitments. We need not be concerned with the hundredth rung or the tenth rung, or even the second rung. Our only concern is with the next rung. Reach for it and leave the rest to your God, but make sure the rungs you choose to climb are close enough to hang on to, or all of your efforts are in vain.

Providence is defined as "The power of God sustaining and guiding human destiny." There is only one way to move providence, and that is to make a commitment. The German poet, Goethe recognized this truth when he shared the following wisdom with us so eloquently:

"Until one is committed, there is hesitancy, the chance to draw back, always ineffectiveness. Concerning all acts of initiative and creation there is one elementary truth, the ignorance of which kills countless ideas and splendid plans: that the moment one definitely commits oneself, then Providence moves too. All sorts of things occur to help one that would never otherwise have occurred. A whole stream of events issues from the decision, raising in one's favor all manner of unforeseen incidents and meetings, and material assistance, which no man could have dreamed would have come his way."

Goethe

"All faith is foolishness,
To a fool."

6

A Handful Of Sand

I'm standing in the back of the auditorium watching the audience while I wait for the Elementary School Christmas program to start. A fellow parent enters, "Good to see you Bill. You never miss one of these things, do you? It's good to see a parent who cares. Talk to you later."

We shake hands and he's gone, off into the world lifting the spirits of everyone he meets with the compliments he gives out so freely. How do I feel about him? I think he's great. I respect him and admire him; I feel good when I'm with him; I would like to be more like him.

Wouldn't it be great to feel good about yourself, to think you're great, to respect and admire yourself; and to feel good when you are with yourself? You can start doing so right now. All you have to do is compliment other people. Treat them as those who make you feel good treat you. You'll hardly believe what happens. Before you know it, the you peering out of your eyeballs will see the positive changes you are making in the lives of others. You will discover that "Hey, he's a pretty nice guy, I think he's great, and I feel great when I'm with him. Hey, will ya look at that, he is me."

The nice part about this process is that you don't have to wallow at the feet of those you admire, and you don't have to become Mr. Nice Guy all at once. You can start gradually, "You look nice today Mary." "I appreciate your help on that project." "Good job, Sam." These aren't big earth-shaking compliments, they aren't major risks, but they are expressions of love.

Begin by complimenting the things people own, then move on to complimenting the way people look. Once you've mastered that, try complimenting things people do and the things they create. It may be a song or a picture, or a job well done. Eventually you will get to the point where you are comfortable complimenting people about who they really are. "I appreciate the way you really care about other people," "I really enjoy being with you," "I love you." It may be riskier, but it is also infinitely more rewarding.

Finally, there comes the unspoken compliment. The magnificent power of a compliment broadcast to the universe through our actions. Last night I was in Seattle, 100 miles from home when my wife called in tears to tell me that my nine year old son Bradley had just been hit in the head with a baseball bat and was on his way to the emergency room with a possible concussion. I had my appointments cancelled and raced home.

When I arrived two hours later, Bradley was asleep in our bed. I sat down beside him and rubbed his back. He became semi-conscious, said "Hi Dad," put his hand on mine, and went back to sleep. I cried. My son is alright. But even more importantly, he knows he is loved. In spite of all my running around and being gone and all of the parental errors I've made over the years, my son knows he is loved. I had the opportunity to give him the ultimate compliment. To let him know that he is important to me; that when it comes right down to it, all the junk I spend my moments worrying about play second fiddle to my son. Our children think we are God for at least the first few years of life. How wonderful it must be to witness God in action loving me.

In an effort to be a better parent, and to make up for some faux pas of the past, I made a conscious effort to compliment each one of my children every day. Then I decided I would do the same for my wife and at least one other person every day. At first it wasn't easy. It didn't feel natural. Sometimes I had to really work to think of someone or something to compliment, but I did it anyway. As with all things, it got easier with practice. Over time I noticed myself being much more aware of the positive all around me because that was what I had become accustomed to looking for. Then I got bolder, and calmer, and before long I found myself laughing in the face of adversity, and seeing the good in every situation. Alright, not every situation – I haven't gotten there yet, but in situations which I once viewed as totally negative.

I now know – although it is not always apparent – that there is positive all around me. People are put in my pathway who allow me the exercise of complimenting them – not because they need the compliment, but because I need to do the complimenting. I intend to continue this strategy until I see a lifter of the spirit of man, and study him in adoration until I realize that "He is Me." I can't imagine how wonderful that will feel.

We can view the world in two ways: a perspective

of eternal light, or a perspective that believes there is a limited amount of everything, including love. This perspective leads to the belief that you'd better hang on to what you've got because you don't have much and you don't want to lose it. People with this perspective act as if everyone is their adversary. They go through life clinging to a handful of sand they call love because they believe there "ain't no more." Their primary concern is holding onto all the sand they can as it slips slowly through their fingers. This perspective only leads to loneliness, depression, and ultimately a spiritual death, if not a physical one. This is the delusion of the world, a mortal misunderstanding. It is the perception we are here to master.

It is faith, and faith alone that can get such death-oriented people beyond the barriers of mortality into the eternal realm where they can see clearly that it is their own self-deception that has brought them to this point.

Faith is the lack of resistance to that which we hope to receive. It is the ability to come to the point where we are willing to at least try the other way, where we are willing to begin passing out our grains of love, trusting that somehow they will be returned to us. As first this will be a terrifying thing to do. This love is what we are. For people of limited perspective, it is actually giving away the last vestiges of their being. But give ourselves away we must. Not only will we have to give away a grain here and there, but if we want to reclaim our entire being we must be willing to dump our entire handful into the bucket of another. In doing so, we have acted contrary to everything our mortal mind has taught us, but we have stepped into a new world of existence. We wake up a new person. We are no longer concerned about the sand in our hand. We no longer look down at the steady stream of our ever-depleting existence.

Instead we look up. We look up to a world of joy, peace, and abundance, a world of light we never imagined existed. It is the world we have been living in all along without recognizing it.

Then one day as you walk along the beach you find a sign posted with your name at the top. It reads: "My dear child, I am overcome with joy that you had the courage and the faith in yourself to pour your love out upon your fellow man. I have been keeping track of the return on your investment; if you would ever like an accounting of your life simply look around you. The love you invested in that first awkward compliment has now multiplied throughout eternity and rather than a handful of dwindling love, your love is as numerous as the sand upon my beaches. Look to your left, look to your right, as far as you can see, and know that my beaches extend beyond the comprehension of your mortal mind, and all that I have is yours. All my honor, all my respect, all my love, — the Universe, is yours."

Not a bad trade I would say.

"Love is the only satisfactory answer
To the problem of human existence."
Erich Fromm

7

Your Gift

T he God within each one of us is a natural creator. Let it express itself and life will be a flowing expression of unbounded joy. Restrain it and your life will be a miserable reflection of the fears you cling to so dearly.

It's not like there is this thing in you that wants to do some creating so the rest of you has to go along to humor it. The thing in you that wants to do the creating is you. It is your vital life force. It is the essence of everything you are when you look beyond that pile of whirling electrons you call your body. If we could understand what we are this would become clear to us — but we can't, at least not in mortal terms, because what we are is not mortal. It does not live on this plane.

The creative energy that is you dwells far beyond your carnal perceptions. It is the power that gives you life; it is the source of your life's vision; it is your sex drive; it is the energy that can lift you to the pinnacle of accomplishment or drag you to the depths of despair. The more of it you are, the more difficult it is to control. It is easy to keep your cart on track when pulled by a gelded pony, but hook up to a half dozen spirited stallions and look out. You're probably going to get pulled around a bit, but when you finally get going in the right direction, you're in for an exciting ride. Sit back and love it.

There is an old Indian philosophy that describes Christ as creative transformation. This idea alone leads me to ponder the importance of expressing our creativity. When you add that "Love is the way", and that God "created" the world, that God is love, all of a sudden creative expression is right up there on the top of the list of self-enhancing things to do because we realize that all creativity is an expression of love.

This doesn't mean you have to become a Rembrandt or a Beethoven or a Frank Lloyd Wright. It simply means to give the gift you're here to give. You might find your bliss in the arts, or you might find it in nursing or gardening or engineering or mechanics or cooking or child-rearing or even in business. The way you will know you have found it is that you will love it. It will be the thing you will most want to do. It may also be the thing you most fear doing because the slams of the world hurt a lot more when directed at your creations — because your creations are you.

Think about the day you first sent your little boy to school on the bus, or the time your teacher hung your picture up in front of the third grade class. There is a mix of emotion at the time. You exposed yourself to the joy in life, but you have also left yourself open to the pain of rejection and failure. Since the beginning of time mankind has been trying to figure out how to have joy without risking pain. Give up. There is no way. Believe me, I've tried everything. There are only two ways to deal with this dichotomy. You can vote for life or you can vote for death. To vote for death is to withdraw into your fears — to avoid the pain by denying life — to not take the chance. To vote for life is to take the chance — to say "I am going to be what I am no matter what anybody says" and then to go out and prove it. This path is the difficult path, the road less traveled, the way of the sage, but it is the only way to "life." Not just figuratively, but actually. Whether you know it or not, your light fades every time you give in to your fears. This light is you, and it will continue to fade until you step up and express your creativity to the world. For some this is easy, for others it will only happen when their flame begins to flicker. For others, it will never happen. They will deny their gift, and thus their very being, under the guise of busyness and excuses and belief in limitations placed upon them, until they slip quietly out of mortality still clinging to their gift.

Too often we have learned not to create because our creations of the past have caused us such pain. You run in to show your mother the horse you just drew and your brother says it's stupid. Then Mommy holds it upside down and says it's about the prettiest tree she's ever seen and Dad asks if he can use your piece of paper to light the fireplace. That hurts, but you get over it, until the coming years when you screw up at the piano recital, the kids laugh at your woodworking project, the dress you made for the prom doesn't fit quite right, people think you sing funny, your parents think all artists are all gay, and your engineering professor says you're stupid for trying to make a perpetual motion machine.

On and on we go, getting slammed for being creative. Yet, what does being creative really mean? It means doing something differently than the way it has already been done. It is these creative pioneers who have created our world for us. They have endured the pain, time after time, until they emerged victorious. Without them we'd still be eating dirt and dragging our women around by the hair. This is where we get our heroes — those who have the guts, or the ability, to tolerate pain enough to dance in the face of ridicule. To do the thing which their fears warn them not to do. Physically or mentally we can learn to do virtually anything that is important to us, yet our fears hold us back — not just from expressing our creativity, but from life itself. We buy into the mortal garbage that says we're too old for ballet, too ugly to act, too dumb to be a composer, too clumsy to dance, and too incompetent to start our own business.

The truth is that the existence of a desire within you is the divine sign that the ability to bring your desire to pass is also within your reach — no exceptions.

Why do you think you're here in the first place? Because God had some stuff left over after he was done making everyone else? The truth is that you are his greatest expression of love. The cutting edge of the Universe. The way the Universe grows is to create. This is true for us too, and for God. We love what we create. Why does God love you? Why do you love your children? I can't answer either of those questions fully, but rest assured that they both have the same answer.

What can you do right now? Sing a song; write a poem; carve a boat; plant a garden; draw a picture; build a kite; design a house; make a sandbox. Just go out and create something that didn't exist before. That is the work of the Gods, and you are a part of the party.

Don't worry about how good it is or isn't. That has nothing to do with anything except the fears of others. It is a creation of yours and is thereby registered in the ether of the universe as an infinitely valuable gift. Don't let anyone ever tell you differently.

There's nothing so sad as a song never sung.
Nothing so lonely as a poem kept to one.
You can fake it and make it — abound to the eye,
But the being that's you knows it's a lie.
So face up to your fears and give what you are.
Knowing inside of it all you're a star.
And whatever your gift be, let it shine through,
And know that this infinite shining is you.

*"People rarely succeed at anything
Unless they have fun doing it."*

La Rochefoucauld

8

Wise Exercise

We all know that exercise will make us feel better in the long run, but we don't do it because it makes us miserable now. In spite of all the warnings from our doctors, in spite of the innumerable physical and emotional benefits we know will occur, we are still not motivated enough to get us to experience the pain now. I think this is a result of a warped sense of the definition of exercise. When I hear the word "exercise" the first things that come to mind are push-ups, military boot camp, or a bunch of jocks bench-pressing the back of a bus. No thanks.

My wife accuses me of doing head-lifts. That's when I lift my head up to see if it's time to get out of bed yet. Actually I'm in pretty good shape, at least I thought I was. I can do 30 or 40 push-ups or run five miles, but I still remember the first day my wife got me to do the Jane Fonda Workout. I thought I was going to die. Nobody is supposed to bend like that. It took me two weeks to stand up straight again.

I guess my father is right. He told me that if you don't enjoy exercising you won't do it. That counts me out. Who wants to suffer now so that they can suffer more later? I'll take it easy now and see what happens. Unfortunately that is the attitude most of us take, and unfortunately what usually happens is that when later comes we wish we would have exercised sooner.

Anyway, the good news is that exercise can be enjoyable and it can make you feel better right now. How do you make exercise enjoyable? I go running down the irrigation canal by our house. The other day my wife revealed to me that it is just as much exercise for her to walk down the canal as it is for me to run down the canal. Impossible, I thought, I come back all sweaty and breathing hard, and she comes back looking like she just walked out of the Spiegel catalogue, and she's smiling. How could it be? A brief review of the laws of physics reveals that she is right. It takes a specific amount of energy to move an object a specified distance regardless of the speed it moves. If you move it faster you just expend the energy in a shorter period of time. This was good news to me. I now run down the canal a little faster than before, and walk back. It's great, I see things I had never noticed before. New animals, new crops, farms I hadn't noticed. Last week I saw some baby eagles contemplating their first leap. I am now truly enjoying my exercise. I look forward to it; I do it more often; and I always feel better when I'm finished.

So find something you like to do, weight lifting, aerobics, yoga, running, tennis, skiing, walking, cutting firewood, anything you enjoy — and do it. Who knows, you might even like boot camp. Another good thing about exercise is that it doesn't have to cost anything. I know, you've chosen water-skiing and you have to buy a boat and a dock and a lake and a house on the water and seven $3,000 water skis, but it doesn't have to be that way. In the first place, it's cheaper to go down to the beach and pay a kid with a boat $500 to take you for a spin than it is to have your own boat. And in the second place, if money is what's holding you back you can choose a different exercise. There are plenty of free recreational facilities in this country. If you can't find one, jump rope or go for a walk. If you can't find a place to walk go in your bathroom and do yoga. Believe me, there is an enjoyable way for you to exercise for no money — right now. Your challenge is to find it, and do it.

Why does exercise make you feel better? It doesn't really matter why as long as it does, but I think there are several reasons.

- It is spiritually empowering to have your mind in control of your body.
- The increased circulation of blood, breath, and lymph fluid has a tremendous cleansing effect.
- It is a good way to get your mind off the burdens you are carrying.
- It makes fear release it's grip on your subconscious mind.
- You will become aware of sensations you had not previously experienced.
- You will experience new people, places, and perceptions.
- Your body will become stronger.
- You become healthier.
- You give yourself a powerful "Live" message.
- It will help you live in the present moment.

- You experience a powerful affirmation of your ability to accomplish things that you once thought impossible.
- You will feel better right now!

So the trick to exercise is simple: find something you like to do, and do it. If you follow this simple plan you will enjoy it while you are doing it, and you'll feel great when you're done. That's enough for me.

9

Extend Yourself

"Extend myself? How in the world am I going to do that? I barely have time to brush my teeth. I mean with school and work and mowing the lawn and training the dog and talking to my wife and kids every two or three days, how am I ever going to extend myself."

Extending yourself doesn't require any more time or any more money and hardly any more effort than you are expending now. And the effort it does require will come back to you 100 fold. How do you do it? You become interested, and you try to help. One way you can tell if you're extending yourself is that it will always involve a little risk, and a little effort. By virtue of making the effort, you are performing an act of love. If it involves a lot of risk and effort you probably won't do it because it's scary to express that much love all at once. That's okay, you aren't expected to. We're only expected to take baby steps. One little extension at a time. As long as we keep stepping, no matter how small the steps, we are making progress. It is only when we stop that spiritual rigor mortis starts to set in. A good signal that it's time to get going again. Here's a list of some possible baby steps you can use to get started:

- Look up
- Say "Hi"
- Ask for what you want
- State what you believe to be true
- Stand up for another
- Take a risk
- Stop to help someone beside the road
- Compliment someone
- Give a speech
- Smile
- Join a club
- Invite someone out to lunch

There is one way I will no longer extend myself. I will never again make a comment to a pregnant woman about her baby. Some guys can do this and get away with it. I cannot. Every time I try it I end up with egg on my face because she's either not pregnant or she had her baby eight months ago. Once again I end up trying to figure out how to play re-do on the last 30 seconds of my life. I must be the only one this happens to. When my wife was only a few months pregnant she was still wearing her Calvin Kleins when the guy at the fireplace store asked her when her baby was due. I couldn't believe it. This guy had guts. I'd rather slay dragons than do what he did. I tried it one more time after his great display of courage and that was it. From now on when I want to make trouble for myself I'm just going to start asking women why they eat so much and get it over with. There is one exception — if she is protruding massively and she's got on one of the T-shirts that says "BABY" with an arrow pointing to her stomach, I will venture forth.

I will also venture forth for my family. The things I will do for them astound me, but it isn't really them who I do it for, it is me. Several years ago I agreed to always coach my youngest child's soccer and basketball teams. I had no idea at the time that I would have four children and this would end up being a ten year commitment. I'm now in my fourth year and have had well over fifty kids on my teams. Then if you add cub scouts, ballet, T-ball, and school programs I end up knowing a whole bunch of these little ones.

I had lunch with my 2nd grader Jessica at the elementary school the other day. When we had finished eating we walked out onto the playground for recess when I heard, "There's Coach, let's get him!" Before I knew it, there were about a hundred little kids pushing and pulling on me with the unified goal of keeping me captive by the tire bridge. I can handle ten or fifteen of them, but this time they had me.

Here I am, a quasi mature adult being bamboozled by a bunch of little kids. At first I considered getting stern with them and insisting that they all let go before they wrinkle my clothes, but the little voice said, "Relax Bill, just go with the flow." For once I listened, and I felt loved. I felt approachable. I felt honored that these micro-masters in the game of life felt so comfortable with me that they would do this sort of thing. Then came the crowning glory. In the midst of the tussle I heard my child exclaim "That's my Dad!" She was so proud to know that the hero of their 11:30 recess world would be kneeling by her bedside in a few hours, stroking her hair, and letting her know that there was nothing more important to her superhero than she was.

It must be nice to have your father be a superhero, for a moment, but very soon they will wake up and find that he is just another being doing the best he knows how to get through this old world. But my blessing, the serendipitous result of extending myself and listening to the still small voice, will be with me — forever.

10

No Bread, No Water

*I*t's easy to be an animal; you've only got two forces at work, your spirit, and your body. The beauty of being an animal is that there is no ego, no rational mind that is capable of being at war with the spirit. The sole purpose of an animal mind is to provide the body with it's needs. Animals are always congruent. They always live in the now. They do not concoct imaginary future disasters and they do not lament about the past. They just exist in the nirvanic ever-present now.

This is where people exist too, but they do not know it. They spend virtually all of their present moments worrying about the future and lamenting the past. The problem is that people have three demands they are always trying to meet which are not always consistent, and they're trying to meet them all at the same time.

For example, your inner being may know that it would be best for you to head home and leave her sitting on the barstool. Your body says no way am I going home, this is going to feel really good. Your mind then goes into analysis paralysis. Yes, this would feel good, but tomorrow it will feel rotten, and besides she might be married, but that doesn't matter anymore, does it? And I wonder if . . . . back and forth goes your mortal mind creating a state we call torment.

Maybe your inner voice says, "Put that down, the last thing you need is another candy bar," your body says, "Oh, but they taste so good," and your mind says, "Well, they do taste awfully good, but I am kind of fat, but just one candy bar won't matter. But then I always say that, one thing is for sure, this one won't matter. What is it going to do, inflate itself and fuse onto my right thigh?" Gulp. Then comes the message. You can't see it, you can't touch it, but you can feel it. Unless of course you've ignored your feelings for so long you've become calloused. Once again you're using logic to battle the forces of another world. You're going to lose every time, until you unsheathe your feelings and send your unseen foes to flight.

The trick is to get your mind, body and spirit all pulling in the same direction. Fasting is one of the best ways of accomplishing this. If you'd like to feel a little better simply decide that you're not going to eat for a predetermined amount of time. None of this forty day stuff. Christ made it, and Ghandi did pretty well, but my guess is you'll end up dead. Twenty-four hours should be long enough, or maybe you'll want to start out by skipping one meal. Make sure that whatever length of time you commit to, you will actually do.

At this point your mind and body are already a little concerned about the potential pain that lies ahead, but they don't think there is even the slightest chance that you will go through with it. Especially since you have let them run your life for so long. They know they're not going to let you follow through on this absurd commitment. Six or seven hours later they begin to realize that you're serious and start sending you distress signals in the form of hunger pangs. This is the test, the refiners fire. You are about to find out who is running your life. Your mortal mind, or the unseen power of the universe. The pain will wane, and it will come again. Don't listen. A few more hours and you will have a new experience. A taste of one of the most powerful experiences you can ever have. You are about to experience the feeling that comes from mastering the illusion and listening to the still small voice. It may not seem like much at first, but it is a major step toward the You you are here to be.

What has happened? You have made a powerful statement about who is running your show, you have kept a commitment in spite of what is sometimes severe pain. You have shown yourself that you can do something that you didn't know you could do. Possibly for the first time in your life your body has learned that it does not have the final say in what goes on.

Now, whenever you start to feel a little less than enthusiastic about life, fast for a day. Before long you'll have those gremlins inside of you all pulling on the same side of the rope. Your spirit has taken a step up to his rightful place as supreme leader. Your mind, which hates losing, is taking its rightful place in the back seat, and your body is pleading with your mind to make sure you feel good all the time because it doesn't want your spirit to torture it any more.

I find it helpful to have a specific purpose about which I fast. It could be a person or issue about which I would like greater clarity, or maybe a fast of gratitude. Although it always improves my internal harmony, having a purpose seems to provide me with an almost quantifiable increase in clarity which leaves me in awe of the unseen powers at work in this world.

It may be a lot easier to be an animal, but I prefer the tortured path of a human being. I don't know why, but sometimes, in between trials, I can hear the still small voice calling out to me that it is all worthwhile. This seems impossible, I can't imagine what good could come from all this struggle. Yet somewhere, deep within my being, I know that I chose this path because it is taking me on the most wonderful adventure directly to my bliss. So I take another step, the scenery doesn't change much, but I know that I am one step closer to home. Then one day I wake up having dreamt a dream. I find myself in a place of perfect peace and I realize it was the dream that got me here. I see that what once appeared to be the action of a vindictive God was really a self-chosen rung in the ladder of my life. "It is all so clear" I think, and in the clarity I start planning my next adventure.

11

Unload Your List

*E*verything you have started or planned or put energy into that you haven't finished is a burden to you. It may not seem that the unwritten letter or the missing molding behind the door are affecting you at all, but they are. It's like a hiker who trims two ounces off his drinking cup, eight ounces off his poncho, half a pound off his sleeping bag, and a pound off his tent. He sprints up the trail with a thirty-pound pack. I end up camping in the parking lot. It wasn't the four cans of Spaghetti O's that did it, it wasn't the two gallons of water nor the "blue-light-special" sleeping bag. I could even handle the four bedroom tent. But all together it wipes me out.

That's the way it is with our "incompletes." No one piece of unfinished business is enough to wipe us out by itself, but all together they drag us down — without us even knowing it. What to do? Make a list of everything in your life that is incomplete. If you have trouble thinking of any ask your spouse, I suspect your stupor will be over. Right now my list looks something like this but it's much longer.

- Put up moldings in the kitchen
- Get the garden ready to plant
- Finish building a go-cart for my kids
- Finish an incomplete in a class I took
- Finish my tax return
- Put our fireplace insert in our fireplace
- Trim the horses feet
- Clean my office
- Fix shower enclosure
- Put up trim in Jonathan's room
- Etc. etc. etc.

I know this list doesn't look like much to you, but to me it's overwhelming — just as your list may appear to be overwhelming to you. It seems like there is no way you could ever get all those things on your list done. The good news is that you are going to be freed from the burden RIGHT NOW! All you have to do is divide these life-sucking burdens up into three categories and you will be free, forever, unless of course you start collecting incompletes again. So take some time to make as complete a list of your incompletes as you can and, when you are done, divide them into the following three categories.

Category #1

Put a number "1" next to a couple of the items that you are going to do right now. Don't try to be super-human and put them all in this category. That could cause a stroke. Just put down a few you can complete today with a little extra effort.

Category #2
Put a number "2" by everything you are going to do, but you are not going to do right now.

Category #3
This is where everything else goes. Put a number "3" next to all the things you really don't have to do, you really don't want to do, and come to think it, you just plain are not ever going to do.

Now for the freedom. Do the incompletes labeled #1, figure out when you will do the things in category #2 and schedule them in your Daytimer — written down, and, here is the fun part — throw away the incompletes labeled #3 because you are never going to do them.

That was easy enough. Now you don't have to carry that hefty backpack around. All you have to deal with are the easy things you have assigned yourself for today. You only have to deal with the other stuff when you get to it, and you never have to deal with the stuff you threw away.

One of the main reasons we get stuck with incompletes is that we don't know what to do. We don't know how much paint to buy, we don't know an address or an angle or a process or a person or something that we allow to hold us up. Don't allow this anymore. You will not always know ahead of time exactly what obstacles lie ahead, and what the solutions will be, but you no longer allow the unknowing to hold you up — you get started anyway. If you run out of paint buy more, if you don't know how to write good letters learn how, or hire someone, or do the best you can and mail it anyway. Do anything to avoid staying stuck. You'll discover that, if you just get started, and focus on the next step rather than the entire project, you'll be finished in no time at all.

Life is meant to flow "Gently down the stream." Gently means going with the flow. Not the massive flow of mediocrity, but the ever-changing flow of your individual life. Incompletes tie you to the past, protect you from your future, and keep you from enjoying the present. How can you live in the flow if you are always paddling around in circles and looking back upstream to where you have been? When we are in the flow, we progress rapidly, moving peacefully from one set of rapids to the next. Not concerned so much with the rapids themselves, but with our ability to run them. Then one day we realize that what once filled our heart with the fear of death is now merely a break in the monotony of the calm.

Eliminating incompletes not only relieves you of a burden, it also makes you feel good every time you see your accomplishment. I had a picture my wife had painted on my desk for over a year. Complete with frame and mat and all the stuff I needed to frame it. After a while I didn't even notice it anymore. One day while attempting to clean my desk I realized how long the painting had been there. "This is driving me crazy" I said out loud, and indeed it was. I got out the ruler, tape and knives, framed it, cleaned up the mess, gift wrapped it and had it waiting for my wife when she got home. She loved it, she thinks I'm the most thoughtful husband in the world, and I feel a little bit like the wonderful husband she thinks I am. The picture now hangs above my dresser and every time I see that compilation of paint, paper, glass and wood I have an entirely different feeling than I did when it was all piled on my desk.

People who don't feel as good as they would like

invariably quote a long list of things they have to do that are burdening them down. They also avoid listing them because they believe such a direct confrontation would undoubtedly be worse than they could possibly imagine and that they would therefore end up feeling even worse than they already feel. The truth is that the major part of our burden comes from not knowing exactly what we are up against — from not knowing our opponent. Our fears run riot with scenarios of failure, rejection, and despair. The other truth is that when we confront the demon face to face he always ends up being much more manageable than our fear-struck mind would ever let us believe.

Make your list, do some, schedule others, and throw the rest away. When do you do this? Right now. Before you read another word. Go ahead, write in this book, I don't care. Just do it right now. Get up and do just one little tiny incomplete, one that will only take a few minutes. Sweep behind the refrigerator, write your grandmother a quick note, scrape the gum off under the table, fix the leaky faucet, make the call you've been dreading. Get up now and throw one of those lousy incompletes out of your backpack. I promise you will feel better if you do, and it won't be a feel better next week or next month; it will be a feel better RIGHT NOW!

*"Man's quest is always for sufficient
Self confidence to be himself."*

12

Free To Forgive

*O*h, the unseen burden of he who cannot forgive another. It pulls him down as an anvil on the neck of a swimming man. He cannot see it or touch it, and he may be so used to it he doesn't even know it is there. But it is, and it is robbing him of his very life moment by moment, until one day he looks back and sees that he has sacrificed his life to hold onto a belief about another that, whether it is true or not, doesn't matter in the least.

Why forgive others? Some people believe you should forgive others because it's mean not to, or because "good" people don't hold grudges, or because the preacher said that God said to. Pure bologna. The only reason to forgive others is because you will feel better. It has nothing to do with the others, it has nothing to do with God, it has nothing to do with heaven or hell or being nice or anything else — it has only to do with you.

In the good book God tells us to leave the judging to him. Not because he wants to be a judge, but because he doesn't want his offspring carrying around such heavy burdens. Judging others is one of the most common spiritual blocks. We go to church and give to the poor and work hard and remain faithful to our wife and do all the external things that "good" people do. Yet when we stop to introspect we find that there are people we want to avoid, people we speak ill of, people who we would like to drag down a little if we could do so without anyone knowing.

Why is this? Why would a perfectly logical, intelligent creature like you and me ever think thoughts that would impede the progress of another? Because we are insecure — period. There is no other reason. When we are secure with ourselves, we have no reason to think or say anything derogatory about another, but when living a lie, no matter how insignificant, we become defense oriented and the success of another becomes a threat to our very being.

You can be sure that whenever you hear someone speaking ill of another or spreading gossip, whether it's true or not, he feels threatened by those who he speaks ill of. Then we learn that others are merely mirrors of ourselves. You cannot love or hate something about another person unless it reflects to you something you love or hate about yourself. That person is in your life to reflect your fears and your feelings back to you. When you begin to use these feelings to guide you in your own self discovery, you will drop your emotional anvil and become grateful for everyone who ruffles your feathers, understanding that whether they know it or not, they are delivering a message from the Universe. A message about yourself that, when heeded, will guide you on the most efficient and effective path to the eternities the world has ever known.

The logic of a grudge holder, which is totally illogical, goes something like this. "All the people in my world are ranked on my mortal scale of intrinsic worth. There are two ways for me to get to the top; one, I can climb up over everyone else to get there, or two, I can pull others down. Yes, that is what I will do. Climbing the ladder takes a lot of effort and risk and who knows what else. I think it will be much easier to just sit here and annihilate those above me. Off he goes taking pot shots at those above him every chance he gets. Occasionally, one of his cohorts falls off the ladder and goes hurling down to the bottom. He takes time out to attend the funeral, but he's back in a few hours trying to knock off someone else. He may appear to be getting to the top when in reality he is denying his true destiny and counter-serving his fellow man. Very shortly his life becomes meaningless, then empty, and before long severe depression sets in. He's not sure why, but he thinks it has something to do with his wife's cooking. Wrong again, he'll make up excuses forever, but until he knows the truth, the truth cannot make him free.

A better analogy of what is really going on is that he and 20 of his friends are trying to pull a truck up a hill. Each man has a bungy cord attached to the front of the truck and is pulling on the other end. The strongest men pull the hardest and as their bungy cords stretch they step out in front of the pack. Then our misguided fool trips them and puts obstacles in their way so he can be in front. Before long he is in front, but he bungled things up so badly that the truck is now rolling down the hill backwards and our friend is the only one denying responsibility.

When Christ said that his purpose was "to bring to pass the immortality and eternal life of man" he wasn't talking about this man and that man to the exclusion of women and children. He was talking about mankind — all of us together. It is the only way it can happen. We're all in this together. I don't care if you're in Siam, Malasia, Tiera Del Fuego, or Hometown U.S.A., you're part of the same game. When we learn how to release our burdens of deceit, greed, and jealousy, our lives become a joy, but only when we begin to forgive others totally and completely can we begin to truly enjoy the unbounded providence of the Universe.

I challenge you for the next 24 hours to make sure that every word that comes out of your mouth is supportive of another human being. Some will find it quite difficult to talk. The first step is to stop the negative flow out, and then in the silence we slowly start the positive chugging along. One word, then another, a kind deed and then two. On and on, building slowly, gaining momentum, line upon line until you find yourself barreling through life with a forgiving heart as your constant companion, and momentum that will never quit. Time will slow, priorities will change, a calm overtakes you, and you find a place of peace that you hadn't known existed.

This may appear easy to do because you don't have to do anything, you just have to stop doing something. The problem is that we are so unaware of our habits that we no longer know we are doing them. It may be helpful to get someone with whom you spend a great deal of time to help you. Get yourself a code word like "Beautiful day" or "May I have a dollar" that your partner says to you every time he catches you about to speak ill of another. You might be giving away a lot of money at first, but I assure you it will be one of the best investments of your life.

Why are we so unwilling to forgive? Because our

grudge allows us to maintain an attitude about another that supports our belief. That's all there is to it. It has nothing to do with the other person. It has everything to do with you. Your unforgiveness is a self-justification of the unjustifiable. It is an excuse you use to justify your unwillingness to face the fears that are keeping you from yourself — a self that would love freely if only it were freed from the ominous fear of self-actualization, the fears of taking total responsibility for yourself, the ultimate fear of presenting yourself to the world confident that you can handle anything that comes your way.

If you are willing to face yourself you will ultimately come to this point. You will eventually take your clothes off on the stage of life unsure of the result. You stand there alone, naked, in silence, awaiting your judgement. You hope and pray for approval, but something more important is taking place. You are becoming one with the Universe. All pretense down, ego aside, nothing but you and the universe. To be rejected at this point would be devastation, total and complete, to be wracked with the pains of hell.

It's okay if your facade is rejected, but this is the real you, the last vestige of your being. Will you survive this ordeal? Yes, you will; it cannot be otherwise. The universe needs you. It cannot survive without you. And it wants the real you unencumbered with the shoulds and oughts and stresses and facades of your past. When you present the real You to the universe you will be wrapped in the unbounded arms of love. You will stand naked in the dark, afraid, alone, tense, awaiting your fate. Silence, darkness, so alone, the moments feel like eternities. You were not struck down immediately so you think there is hope, and in the hope you relax, and as you relax you release, and in the release you win. You win the victor's crown, you walk where the Savior walked, for you have mastered fear and doubt. As the lights come up you see that you have become the most glorious entity in the universe — Yourself.

13

Your Helping Hand

O ne of my perennial jobs every winter is to stack
the firewood. I don't hate it, but I don't cherish
those moments either; I just do it. Recently I was
visiting some friends out of town and I had five
or six hours with nothing scheduled. I looked around for
something to do and found a pile of firewood that needed
to be hauled into the basement and stacked.

For some reason I actually enjoyed stacking my
friends' wood. It seemed rather odd to me at first to be getting a degree of joy from doing something that I usually
begrudged. What was the difference? Their wood was cut
into larger pieces, it was wet, it was heavier, it was slimy,
there were slugs on it, it had to be hauled into the basement
instead of just stacked, and I didn't have gloves. Nothing
on the physical plane could explain my attitude. Then I
thought about the time that Rob VanHalder had split and
stacked my firewood while I was gone. I came home all

wrapped up in my usual thoughts of too much to do and all the other junk I think about while trying to get through the day, and suddenly I realized that something was different. The pile of wood next to my house was gone! Not only was it gone, it was split and stacked neatly where it is supposed to go. I couldn't believe it! Who could have done such a thing?

Anyway, I felt loved. All my jangled feelings flowed right out of me. I realized that while I was out jousting with the world a fellow jouster was hard at work helping me without any reason other than to help me. He gave the man with everything the one thing he really needed at that time. Love disguised as a stack of firewood.

No wonder I enjoyed stacking that wood. I was giving another person the feeling I had years ago. I was giving them a few more moments to spend doing the things they really enjoy. I was giving them a gift for no logical reason. In my own feeble way I was expressing my love to them as a wise man did to me many years ago.

§§§

When I finished writing this section yesterday it was the shortest section in the book which didn't seem appropriate seeing as helping others is fundamental to feeling good. It was a beautiful sunny day so I decided that a short section was okay. I would quit for the day and go for a run down the canal as I often do. As the universe always does when we aren't in there bungling things up, I was given what I needed at the time.

I ran down the canal through the back of farms and forests and a game preserve miles from anywhere. I ran past the forest and the bee tree, past the baby ducks and the hawks all the way to the "big bridge" where I frequently stop to rest and think. For some reason I jumped over the fence beside the canal and walked through the trees along a creek where I stopped for a while and leaned against a half fallen tree to rest and cool off.

After a minute of enjoying the beauty, I noticed a small glob of afterbirth right beside the creek. Looking around I found the forlorn mother cow still trailing the rest of the afterbirth. I looked around some more and there was not a calf anywhere to be found. This was odd, it couldn't have been born more than 10 or 15 minutes ago. Ten feet further down the creek the water had washed the dirt out from under the roots of an elm tree leaving roots that protruded three or four feet over the surface of the water from the other side of the creek. To my horror I could see the body of the newborn calf stuck underwater by the tree roots. What a shame I thought, he was born into this beautiful world, he tried to stand up and stumbled as we all do, but he fell into the creek and drowned. Ten minutes and his sojourn was over. I climbed down the bank to the water's edge and peered under the roots. There was three or four inches of space between the roots and the water where, to my surprise, I saw the nose and eyes of one frightened little creature pressed tightly up against the bottom of the roots. I jumped in the creek and pulled a scared, slimy, cold little calf out from under the water. I could hardly believe he was alive. I picked him up the best I could, stumbled up the bank and laid him down on the grass in the sunshine.

The poor little guy was shaking so badly I still wasn't sure he would make it. I squeegeed all the water I could off of him with my hands, assured him that everything would be fine, and left him to his mother. She walked by still dragging afterbirth, gave him a sniff, and left for the other side of the pasture. Great, his mother didn't recognize him anymore because his scent was washed off in the creek.

What am I going to do? If I leave him here the coyotes will get him, I can't carry him home, and I can't stay out here all night. Plan B — I scraped a little bit of afterbirth up with a stick and rubbed it all over the little guy, then I ran over to the other side of the pasture and chased his mother back. She could care less. She looked in the creek, made a few cow noises and started walking away. Fortunately she walked by the little guy and gave him one more sniff. It worked! She started licking him, and licking him, and pushing him all around with her tongue. I thought the battle was won, but the little guy was just too weak. Calves usually stand up within minutes, but he didn't have the strength. With each passing minute his efforts seemed more futile.

"Please little guy, stand up, the sun will set soon and you will not make it through the night if you don't stand up now," I whispered. He seemed to sense my urgency and with every ounce of energy in his trembling little body he got the back half up and a minute later was finally on all fours. He stood there trembling three feet from the milk of life. To drink was life; to not drink meant he would never see a sunrise. There was nothing I could do, but nature, in her infinite wisdom can do anything. The mother took one step closer, the calf took one wobbly step, then another, and finally the milk of life warmed his belly.

There were tears in my eyes. Me, a hard boiled, totally logical, adult human being crying because a cow got some milk. I sat in the pasture for a while thinking about this. I did the only logical thing, anyone could have done it. Baby cows die every day, yet somehow this one was special. It was special because I loved it, and I grew to love it in the same way we grow to love our children and everything else in this world, by taking risks and expending effort for them. It is an incredible thing we will never fully understand, but when we help others we begin to love them and when we love them we become one with them. And as we become one we feel an incredible warmth develop deep within our being. This is the process of unification. Not just unification of you with the universe, but unification of the universe with itself.

Now, you may be thinking that it is a good thing that I came along, or that the calf should be grateful to me, or that I am a wonderful guy, but as always, the world we perceive is the reverse of the actual world. The truth is that I wasn't there for the calf, the calf was there for me. I may seem like a hero, I even felt like one for a moment, until I became aware of the truth that the Universe will always provide what we need, and that it does indeed work in strange ways.

I needed to pull that calf out of the creek, I needed to witness the calm acceptance of this doomed creature in his last moments, I needed to participate in the bringing to pass of a miracle. The chances of that calf living another ten minutes were less that 100 million to one, yet he lived. I get all bent out of shape if I don't know how I'm going to pay the bills or fix the car or do the endless list of unimportant things I've got to do. The Universe knows so much more than I; why on earth don't I have the calm faith of a newborn calf?

So I walked home soaking wet, slimy, dirty, smelling like a cow, but I felt great. I was smiling inside, humming a tune, infinitely more aware of the beauty all around me. The air was fresher, the trees more awesome, even my body seemed lighter and more agile, yet nothing had changed except I had helped another. I had given a gift of myself to a nameless cow and I was reaping the immeasurable reward. After all these years I will finally admit that Santa Claus was right. It does indeed make you feel a whole lot better to give than to receive.

14

Laugh Out Loud

"Mine is to teach men to despise death and to go on in fearless majesty, annihilating self, laughing to scorn thy laws and terrors, shaking down thy synagogues as webs."

William Blake

"*L*augh? That's easy for you to say, but if you were me it wouldn't be so easy."

"Laugh anyway."

"But what is there to laugh at?"

"There's lots to laugh at, but even if there isn't, laugh anyway."

"How can I laugh if there isn't anything to laugh at?"

"Fake it, Ha - Ha - Ha. It will make you feel better. I bet if you fake it in public you'll have something to laugh at."

So many of us have interpreted the teachings of the good book to mean not to laugh, and to live a life of solemn austerity. I call that a misinterpretation. Remember the good book also says that there is a time for all things, including a time to laugh. When is that time? For me it is just about anytime I take myself too seriously. I get all stressed out about this deadline and that obligation and how important all of my doings are, and before long I'm a miserable bag of nerves. One look at reality — a child tying her shoe, the miracle of my eyeball, or a glimpse of how infinitely important my 1993 tax return is in the eternities — and I have to sit back and laugh — at myself. What is so important that it should preclude laughter from my life? Nothing. Absolutely, positively nothing. If you find that you aren't laughing very often you can be sure that you are taking yourself, and your life, a little too seriously.

"But life is a serious matter" you say. Unfortunately that is true for many people. They have come to the deluded conclusion that there is some honor in carrying around burdens that they have been "commanded" not to carry. They also believe that the "nose-to-the-grindstone-be-responsible-for-everything" approach works better than the "do-what-I-can-this-moment-and-smile" approach.

It is not noble to suffer, it is foolish. This does not mean that I don't ever suffer, or that people with challenges are fools. It simply means that those who choose to suffer because they think it is noble or righteous or macho, or whatever delusion they have that keeps them from laughing, are foolishly throwing away their precious moments of eternity in exchange for a mirage. These "responsible" souls mistakenly believe that their value to the world is directly correlated to their ability to nobly do what is

"Right" in the face of all adversity. I guess they have their place, but if I were stuck on a deserted island I wouldn't want one of them around.

This does not mean that you've got to start spending more time getting juiced at the pub. This is definitely conducive to laughter, but it is an induced laughter. You've got to learn to laugh at yourself right here, right now, wherever you are, whatever you are doing. I'm not suggesting that you live your life in a state of continuous, riotous laughter, but that you approach life as a kind of game and sit back and watch yourself play. When you can gain that perspective you might spend a little time crying at first, but you will also have plenty to laugh about — forever.

I keep a 3 x 5 card catalogue of interesting, humorous, or noteworthy things that happen in our family. If I ever lose so much perspective that I can't think of something to laugh about a quick browse through my cards will get me straightened out. Here's one:

There I am on the court with my team of five-year-old basketball stars. Zero to zero. Twenty seconds to go, the Fighting Frogs shoot, and miss, and we get the rebound. The crowd goes wild, a long pass up court and who should catch it but my son Jonathan. A couple more bounces and he will be in position for what could be the only basket in the entire game when — his gum falls out of his mouth.

What do you do when you're five years old, your Coach / Father has laid down the law about gum chewing, every eye is on you, the fans are screaming, your team is counting on you, you can't stop bouncing the ball, and your little wad of gum is staring up at you from the foul line?

One instant of panic, two dribbles with his left hand, he picks up the gum with his right, pops it back into his mouth, chews twice, and scores! The spectators roar and clap, and laugh 'till they cry, and Jonathan gains a place in the annals of Ellensburg history.

No matter how important I think I am, reliving that incident puts me back in my place every time. I also start laughing every time I think of my sister trying to tell a joke. Not because her jokes are funny. I have no idea if they're funny or not. It's because she thinks they're so funny she breaks up before she can even get the first word out and she laughs hysterically until she can't breathe while we wait in suspense ready to do CPR. They must be really good jokes; maybe I'll get to hear one someday.

If you can't think of anything to laugh about, do something stupid. Wear plaid pants, sing a song at work, go swimming with your clothes on, or keep a secret from everyone. If everything is getting too serious write your cantankerous boss an anonymous love letter, short sheet your own bed, or wear your underwear backwards. Then, when the heat is really on, your boss is after you, your wife has had it, and the IRS is at your door, just think to yourself. "Right buddy, you might think all this is pretty important, but I want you to know that right now as we speak I've got my underwear on backwards." Absurd, yes, but it will make you laugh inside and it will take the clench out of any situation.

If you haven't laughed for a while, or if you'd like to laugh a little more, try a couple of these:

- Read a joke book
- Listen to a Bill Cosby tape
- Close your eyes and think of the funniest things that ever happened to you
- Go watch kids play in a park
- Put on the ugliest clothes in your closet
- TP (toilet paper) your neighbors house (or your

boss's)
- Watch home movies of you as a kid
- Watch your home movies backwards
- Help in a Kindergarten class
- Scratch a poodle's stomach until his shaking leg gets him bouncing all over the place

So simple, so impractical, and yet so powerful. Without the absurd our life can become drudgery rather than a magical journey of discovery. Yet what good is the absurd if we do not recognize it all around us? When life is so serious that we forget to laugh, something is seriously wrong. Take a moment to look around you and you will find something to laugh about. If you don't, take a look at yourself and surely you will find that the absurd dwells right there inside you with the kingdom of heaven.

o   o   o

A peacock just walked by my window and the minute size of its brain in comparison with its transcendent beauty reminded me of the man who asked his wife why in the world God made women so beautiful and so dumb. His wife explained that God made women beautiful so men would love them, and he made them dumb so they would love men. Surely we all are one.

I laugh at doubt and greed and fear,
    And watch them slowly disappear.
I joke with guile and lust and hate,
    And in the distance watch them fade.

Though they try, there is no pain
    My laughter will not cure.
My shield and sword and joust and spear,
    My saving grace for sure.

So when the depths of hell my fears,
    So nearly have me banished.
As I look them in the eye and laugh,
    Their searing flames all vanish.

So laugh and laugh and laugh again,
    And go your merry way.
For only when you've laughed out loud,
    Will you have lived today.

15

Learn Something New

ou mean go back to school? No, that's not what I mean. I mean learn something. You can learn something in school, but there are lots of other ways. Ask someone, read a book, take some contraption apart, fix something, watch a worthwhile program on TV, or just contemplate for a while. You will be amazed at the knowledge that is already in you waiting to be accessed.

Let's try it right now. How do they make the hole down a hypodermic needle? Bonnie told me yesterday that they roll a piece of flat metal into a tube and weld the seam. Wasn't that fun! Okay, how about this. There are over 500,000 trombone players in the United States; 85 percent of adult cat owners are women. The chances of a vegetarian dying of heart disease is 14 percent compared with 50 percent for the general population. That was easy trivia stuff, but it still counts if you've learned something.

For some real fun, read the encyclopedia or check out some books at the library. Not only will you feel better you will also become more interested, and much more interesting. How about some history? Did you know that the great conqueror Cortez was almost killed by a woman who threw a plant pot at him from a balcony and hit him in the head? The way he escaped that fate was to order one of his men to run him through with his sword so that people wouldn't say that he was killed by an old woman.

Why do we feel better if we learn something? I think it is because we are curious creatures. It is our natural tendency. That's why little kids get into everything. Unfortunately, we usually get the curiosity beat out of us by the time we are five feet tall. I think John Denver said it best in his song I Want To live:

> *"I want to see, I want to know,*
> *I want to live, I want to grow . . ."*

What is life other than a process of gaining new knowledge and applying it? When we are actively engaged in this process we are alive. We are like a little child, curious, present, persistent, and forever trying something new, living in a world of wonder. When we are not engaged in this process we are on the conveyor belt to the grave.

This knowledge can come from watching your grandchild play in the leaves, or sitting in quiet meditation. It can come from attending class or watching a bug crawl across your arm. You learn something new every time you do something or think something that you haven't done or thought before. Isn't that what life is all about? Why would you want to live if you weren't having new experiences?

Another benefit of learning something new is that while you are learning something new your mind is distracted from the fears that constantly beset your mortal mind. Your mind cannot think of two things at once. It can flit back and forth pretty fast, but it can't think about two things at once. Therefore, if you immerse your thoughts into what you are learning or experiencing, these moments have been denied to the fear-generating portion of your cerebral cortex and you experience an additional moment of bliss. And what is a life of bliss but a whole bunch of blissful moments lined up one after another.

Whoever said that knowledge is power was forgetting something. Knowledge is only potential power. It only becomes power when you use it.

An eager young agricultural extension agent was driving down a country lane when he spotted a farmer plowing his field the "old way." He immediately pulled over, climbed the fence and ran out to tell the farmer about the findings of the new furrow direction studies. The farmer pulled his tractor to a stop to see what the young man wanted. The agent excitedly recited his knowledge of furrow direction, water retention, and about the increase in crop yield that could be easily attained. When the agent finished speaking the old farmer looked him in the eye and said "Son, why would I care about that stuff? I ain't farmin' half as good as I know how to now."

How often do we live our lives like the old farmer. Knowing what to do, but too comfortable with the old way to bother making any changes. Yet these changes are invariably the key to living the rich, full life we are here to lead. Just learning something new will make you feel better, but if you were to ever apply it to your life, you'll hardly believe how much better you'll feel having the

Universe smiling down upon you.

Several months after my seventeenth birthday I was working as the quality control supervisor at a remote cannery in Alaska. Sitting in my ramshackle office I was frequently visited by a young Eskimo man named Walter, while I measured can seams. One day after watching me work for a while Walter said, "I would give anything to be a Kass'aq." Which in English means "I would give anything to be a white man."

"Why" I asked "would you want to be a Kass'aq?"

"Because Kass'aqs are so smart and they know so much and they can do anything they want." Walter then explained that Kass'aqs can figure things out and fix things and they always know what to do. Underlying all of his observations was the insinuation that Eskimos cannot do these things, and they cannot do anything they want. In some respects Walter was right. He was not as free to do as much as I, and the other few Kass'aqs could do. While there were undoubtedly other issues involved, the two main factors limiting Walter were his self-perception, and his lack of knowledge. Both within his power to change, and unlike most of us, change he did.

I invited Walter into my office and assured him that he could do anything I could do if he just learned how. He didn't believe that was possible but he was so eager to learn he decided to give it a try. That day I showed him how to measure can seams with a micrometer. I explained botulism, and taught him how to check a retort temperature graph. Within a week he had it mastered and was back for more. How does this machine work? What if it isn't hot enough? Why do you test three cans? On and on he drilled me, until by the end of the summer, when I left to start college Walter knew more about quality control than anyone in the cannery. Incredible, never have I seen a person so resolute and persistent in his pursuit of knowledge. Several years later I received a letter. Walter, who once had a difficult time reading and writing, had been admitted to the University of Alaska, and let me tell you, he feels great!

"Man is God afraid."
Maeterlinck

16

A Look Within

I know the dogmatists aren't going to like this one. They believe that there is this big guy in the sky called God with a stick, a bank, a dating service, and a doctor kit. They believe that God is up there listening to all of our prayers and deciding if we get what we have asked for or not based on how "good" we've been. They think that if we pray "hard enough" it will help; if we pray enough times he might hear us, and then who knows what he'll do anyway. Dogma, Dogma, Dogma!!! A sure path to neurosis.

What they don't understand is that "Prayer changes man, not God." We are the ones who determine if our prayers are answered, not God. God does not decide if our prayers are answered, he does not judge us, and he does not punish us, nor does he even care in the least whether we live or die. All he does is love us. And that is all we really want from him. If we could feel for a moment the intense love of the divine, nothing else would matter. Isn't that incredible? Just feeling love would take all the pain out of relationships, debt, fear, loneliness, illness, death, and every other self-inflicted torture device of man. It is incomprehensible to us that we are loved so much that we are a part of a system that proclaims, in the words of the Master, "Whatsoever you ask believing, you shall receive" or "Before ye call, I shall answer." Dear children, the answer is Yes, you can have whatever you want — period. You pay with belief.

Think of it like this. God said to his children, "Children, who would like to go to a wonderful playground and do anything you want?" Of course most of us jumped for joy. "Before we go though, I'd like you all to go to the Celestial Mega Mall and get anything you want and put it on my account. Then, put it all in a bag and put your name on it. I'll give it to the playground supervisor and anytime you want something from your bag just tell him and he'll get it for you. Also, if you ever want anything that you forgot to pick up at the Mall just let him know and he'll get it for you. Okay?"

"You bet" we said — and he took all his children to the playground.

"I'm going golfing for a while," God said to the playground supervisor. While I'm gone, give my kids anything they want." He turned to us. "I'll be gone for a bit kids, if you need anything ask the playground supervisor. He'll be up on the roof of the gymnasium with your bags. Just holler up to him and he'll throw down anything you want." And God left. Well, he didn't really leave, he just stepped aside to watch us play.

At first we didn't do too well. We got cold and sick and frustrated because we ran out of things. We'd talk about the guy on the gymnasium roof, but no one really believed it. Yet, every once in a while some kids would get so sick or cold or depressed they would drag themselves over to the gymnasium, and we don't know exactly what happened, but they'd return with a blanket or a toy, or their disease would be gone. "A miracle" we would say, "why don't any miracles ever happen to us?"

We were sure that miracles were a thing of the past, yet every now and then a few of us would stand over by the gymnasium and holler a bunch of vague orders up and then we'd run away feeling stupid, knowing for sure that there is no one up there taking orders. There may have been years ago, but he's probably a pile of bones by now. The truth is that it takes the Playground Supervisor a few seconds to get the stuff out of our bags. Usually by then we've changed our order or had run away in disbelief.

This reminds me of the Sunday School teacher who was giving a lesson on prayer. She asked the children how many of them have ever prayed sincerely — all the hands went up. Then she asked how many pray sincerely 50 percent of the time — about half the hands went up. How many of you pray sincerely 75 percent of the time — five hands remained up. How many of you pray sincerely 90 percent of the time — two or three hands were still raised. How many of you pray sincerely every single time? Only Bobby had his hand up. Disbelieving, she asked Bobby to explain to the class how he was able to pray sincerely every single time. "It's easy" replied Bobby, "I only pray when I'm in deep trouble and I need help fast."

Unfortunately this is the attitude most of us take. We think of prayer, or looking within, as a last ditch effort to try when all else has failed, rather than building a trusting relationship with the divine. That is the purpose of prayer — and meditation — and yoga — and Tai Chi — and mantras — and church — and all the mental gymnastics we love-seeking mortals employ to learn to let the love of the Universe into our lives. I know this sounds sort of theosophical, the kind of thing you might hear a preacher screaming from the pulpit. But it is the fundamental basis of human spiritual growth, and it doesn't have anything to do with religion or sin or any of the other dogma we let get in our way. It only has to do with recognizing the divine within ourselves.

The way to find it is to look within, and whatever you want to call it, the way to look within is to meditate. To turn off your frantic, whirling mortal mind and let the still small voice from within reach your heart. This is often difficult because we have been programmed to search for ourselves out there rather than within, but as the good book says, "The kingdom of heaven is within."

Looking within does not consist of reciting a list of your desires to an unseen Santa Claus. Like meditation it is a chance to become more intimate with yourself. How do you meditate? There is no "correct" way, but it is helpful to go to a place where you will not be distracted, get comfortable, either shut your eyes or focus on one point. Then stay like that for a while. Watch your mind at work. Become a detached observer of your thoughts. It might take a while at first because your mind naturally resorts to its frantic whirling concerns of the day. Be patient with yourself. If you just sit there and wait, you will eventually come to the place where you are living purely in the here and now — a place where you have a laser-clear perspective of your life; a place where you see yourself as you really are, and where you always know what to do. Isn't that really what all your prayers are about anyway?

There are as many ways to meditate as there are people, but basically you are going to peek in on your inner self, to take a moment to connect with the divine and to recognize the miracle that you are.

This is what Christ meant when he said "Peace I give unto you, not peace as the world knows that is here today and gone tomorrow, but an everlasting peace . . . " a peace that will make you feel better than anything you had ever imagined possible.

Where is the prize? Whenever I am trying to find something I think of the one who hid it. What are their characteristics, how do they think, how hard do they want this search to be. So, where would God hide the prize? If he put it in a particular country, or religion, or time period we could spend our entire lifetime searching in vain. God wouldn't do that. God would hide it someplace obvious, a place each of us can find wherever and whenever we are. Sure enough, that is exactly what he did. He hid it in the only place there is that is always accessible to each of us. Have you ever searched frantically for something only to find that you are holding it in your hand?

"In the tender leaf
Lies the wisdom of the ages."

17

Nature's Way

"Nature is the only perfect analogy of reality."

Nature teaches us all things. Not only does she teach us all things, she will draw all the negative emotion right out of our being, if we will let her. We act like a kid who has been naughty waiting for Dad to get home. We can't sit still. We fidget and wiggle and think about all the junk that we have to deal with and we don't let nature in, but if we just sit there long enough, our mind will eventually run out of distractions and the peace comes. This is not just a therapy for manic depressives, it is a way for any of us to feel better right now. Some of the most peaceful people I know spend most of their day in nature, and they still can't get enough. Why not? Because there is never enough, just one continuous path of feeling better and better and better each day — day after day, week after week, month after month, year after year, eternity after eternity. No wonder people shoot each other on the Los Angeles freeway; they haven't seen a tree in years.

Not only will nature put you at peace, she will put your children at peace too. On a recent trip to Seattle we were sightseeing with our four rambunctious young children. They were so excited, we couldn't get even one of them to stop talking for a moment. Rather than laying down the law and threaten bodily injury or gross privilege deprivation, as is my first tendency, we used the nature trick. We took them to Volunteer Park and let them run all over the lawn and climb trees for a half hour, then we took them to the conservatory, a large glass building containing every kind of plant imaginable. We entered in awe. Our four little bundles of energy became so engrossed in the biological wonders they didn't say a word except to call one another over to see a particularly beautiful or unique specimen. Our two-year-old, Ryan, stood by the fish pond pointing and whispering "Fishy" to every passerby. Jonathan, our five-year-old, was awed by the poky things in the Cactus room. Jessica couldn't get enough of the flowers, and Bradley wanted to add a jungle room on to his bedroom. When we finally drove away the mood in our car had changed from one of chaos to one of tranquility and wonder. Four little spirits trying to grasp the eternal wonder that created us all.

How do you get close to nature? In as many ways as you can. Touch it, smell it, see it, feel it, taste it, lay on it, bury yourself in it, eat it. You could also:
- Take a hike
- Plant a garden
- Walk on the beach
- Swim in a lake

• Climb a tree
• Plant some flowers
• Eat outside
• Walk in the park
• Pick berries
• Sleep under the stars

Or best of all, listen to it — listen beyond the chirping birds and gurgling creeks and it will quiet your mind until something inside you finally gets the message. The message will come as an inner peace, a knowing, an understanding that you are indeed an integral part of an eternal plan so immense, so divine, and so loving that your mortal mind will never comprehend it. You will understand that not only do you need the universe, the universe needs you. You are part of the puzzle. Even with all your imperfections you are filling a divine role right this moment that no one else could ever fill.

We are nature too. We forget this sometimes. We tend to think there are three kinds of things in the universe. Things God made, called nature; things we made, called stuff; and Us. We forget that God made us too, and that everything we make we make out of the "stuff" God gave us. Not only did He make us, he made us just like him. He also gave us this great playground and all these toys and billions of playmates. What else could a cosmic child of the Universe ever want?

How do I connect with nature? I like to sit out by our pond and watch the Koi fish. It reminds me that there is so much more to my world than I am aware of. It's a feeble example, but sometimes I feel like God. I see these beautiful creatures confined to my pond who are unaware of a greater reality. I see them squabble about food. I watch them come to the surface when the sun shines. I see their personalities. Some always stay in the group, some like to go off on their own. Big Blue is always off on his own. Maybe it's because he's a different color than the rest. Who knows, but he has grown bigger that the other fish. As for me, I don't care what they do I just take care of them and enjoy their beauty.

Probably my favorite way to be in nature is to run down the canal by my house early in the morning. I've done it a thousand times yet it is never the same. I see eagles and ducks and blackbirds soaring through the sky. The canal feeding the plants, the plants feeding the cows, and the cows feeding man. Then I come to a cow skeleton and I am brought face to face with my own mortality. There are the burnt trees reaching for the sky and the dead trees feeding the tender undergrowth. This time of year there are baby ducks, skunks, cows, birds, new corn and hay, and water flowing everywhere. In a few months this will be snow and brown and ice — the appearance of death, pregnant with the beauty of another season. I turn to the impending sunrise and walk home knowing in the depths of my being that I am loved by an unseen creator of life more perfect and powerful than I can possibly imagine — and in this knowing I walk in peace.

18

You Can Relax Now

"**R**elax? Are you crazy? How am I supposed to relax? I'm behind at work, my wife is sick, the kids are driving me crazy, the lawn is three feet tall, and I have no idea how I'm going to pay the bills. That's easy for you to say relax, but if you had problems like me it wouldn't be so easy."

"So what are you going to do?"

"I have no idea what I am going to do, that's the problem. If I knew how to get out of this mess I wouldn't be so stressed out about it, would I?"

"That's why I said relax."

"You don't get it, do you? How am I supposed to relax with all this craziness going on?"

"Does being stressed-out make it easier?"

"No, I don't know, but there's not much I can do about the stress until I get all these problems solved. I mean how am I supposed to relax when the bill collectors are knocking at my door and I've got to work ten or twelve hours a day and . . . . ."

"Excuse me for interrupting, but you've got it backwards."

"I've got what backwards?"

"Everything, typical human. For some reason your species seems to think that peace will come when the problems are solved rather than knowing that the problems will solve themselves when we get to peace."

"What? What are you talking about? Are you some sort of crazy mystic dude or something?"

"No. I'm just like you, but I know more. Would you like me to explain it to you?"

"I don't know, I guess so. I still think you're crazy but it can't hurt to listen."

"Please do listen. You see, what is, is. That will always be. The only thing that varies is your perception of what is. Let me illustrate.

A mother and her son walk a wooded path; a snake slithers across their way. The mother shrieks in horror, the son lunges after his new-found challenge — same woods, same path, same snake, different perception.

Two men burdened by the cares of the world. One frantically trying to solve his problems, the other taking one calm step at a time knowing that the door to his dreams opens inward."

"What does that mean?"

"That means that the door to the place you want to go opens inward, towards you. It means that the harder you push against the door, the tighter it closes. It means that you will never get to your illusive goal until you relax and step back from the door. When you do, you will find that it will swing open of its own accord. The only thing that has been holding it shut has been your pressure. Do you understand?"

"Yes, I get the part about the door, but how do I take the pressure off?"

"Do you remember the part in the Wizard of Oz where it snows on the poppy fields and Dorothy wakes up and she skips away singing about the Yellow Brick Road?"

"Yes."

"Who does she skip away with?"

"The Scarecrow, the Lion and the Tin Man. Oh, and her dog is with them too."

"Right, that is taking the pressure off."

"What is taking the pressure off?"

"Thinking about something else. When we started talking about the Wizard of Oz your door started to open because you weren't thinking about all your pressures. But the moment your thoughts came back to this room it slammed shut again. What you have to understand is that you lead yourself through your life by your thoughts. What you think is where you go. No exceptions, no variation. It is possible that when you wake up in the morning your wife will be feeling better, your neighbor will offer to mow your lawn, and you'll get a promotion at work that will pay more and require less time isn't it?"

"I guess it's possible, but it isn't very likely."

"The point is that there are billions of wonderful possibilities that could happen right now but you are holding the door to them shut because you won't relax. The problem is that your consciousness is down in a hole seeing only one possibility, continued struggle. That's all you can see, and therefore it is all you think about, and therefore that is all you get. Focusing on your problem keeps you in a harried state, which keeps you in the hole, so that you can't see anything else. The stress attaches you to your problem as if it were a permanent fixture in your life rather than one fleeting condition that will never appear the same again. Besides, the universe is beckoning to you, telling you what to do. But you can't hear her because she speaks so softly. If you will just relax, quiet your mind, think of the beauty all around you, and the blessing you have of inhaling your next breath, you will very shortly know exactly what to do. You see, the Universe has a much greater perspective than you do. From your hole you see one option. From ground level you will see hundreds, from the top of the trees you would see thousands, and from the Universe's perspective the options are truly unlimited."

"The Universe will tell me what to do?"

"The Universe is already telling you what to do. She has been doing so all along, the problem is that you don't listen, or else when you do your logical mind can't see why pulling over to the side of the road, or calling Mary, or whatever it is you are being guided to do has anything to do with anything. The truth is that each of these seemingly absurd directives would have gotten you where you want to go more directly than you could ever imagine. You see, Mary's brother-in-law owns two-thirds of the company you work for, and the man that owns the other third would have pulled over to the side of the road to see if you need help. Either meeting would have put your hat in the ring for the new position of Director of Overseas Marketing which incidentally pays more than twice your current salary and would give you complete control of your schedule. But Nnnoooo — I can't see why it's going to do me any good from my hole, so I'm not going to do it."

"You're kidding me, I remember that, calling Mary

and pulling over, that was the universe telling me to do those things. I can't believe it. How did you know."

"Just remember two things Bill — if you relax, you will always know what to do, and when you know what to do, you will always feel better. Now repeat after me: My ship comes in over calm seas, my ship comes in over calm seas, my ship comes in over calm seas."

"My ship comes in over calm seas, my ship comes in over calm seas, my ship . . ."

I sat straight up in bed. What a dream. It was dark but I grabbed a pencil and piece of paper and wrote it down. The Universe had truly spoken.

o   o   o

We tend to think that we can accomplish something of our own accord. The truth, the best I can explain it is that we are totally powerless. The only way we can accomplish anything is to invoke the assistance of the angels. I tried to do it my way for years. I prayed and pondered, I tithed and cursed and begged and pleaded. I tried everything, to no avail. Then one night in a dream I learned that angels don't speak English. They were there all the time trying to figure out what I wanted, but they too were totally frustrated because they could make no sense of my erratic behavior. "You've got to show them what you want" was the counsel of my night-time phantasm. No wonder I wasn't getting anywhere; the angels didn't know what I wanted. So I showed them. I figured that if I was going to show them what was most important to me I would have to do it everyday, and I would probably do it first, and I would let other things wait until I got it done. For sure the angels would catch on if I did those three things. Sure enough they did. And sure enough, before I knew it, my dream had become reality. The funny thing was that it almost seems as if I did it myself. If I hadn't tried so hard to do it myself for so many years I could probably still fool myself. But now I know better.

19

A Song To Sing

*T*hey all do it. Every organization whose mission is the spiritual growth of mankind has a song. The Christians have Hymns, the Indians Chant, the Krishnas have mantras, the Children of Israel have Psalms, but the purpose is the same – to raise the consciousness of mankind.

It is not coincidence that song is practiced by people on all four corners of the earth. Nor is it the result of a commandment giving God who has dictated to the spiritual leaders of the world that song will be a part of their dogma. Rather it is a result of people doing what works. It is a result of people striving to find their higher self because it feels good, and finding that song helps them to get there.

Not only does song expand you as an individual, song also brings people and nations closer together. This past summer my oldest son Bradley had the opportunity to sing in a Japanese / American children's choir. Two groups of children from opposite sides of the world practiced the same songs for several months. The Japanese students then traveled to our town and together they put on a delightful presentation for the community. The concert was great, especially the finale where the children circled the room hand-in-hand singing "It's a small, small world." There wasn't a person in the audience who wasn't touched. The children didn't know it, but somewhere deep within the minds of the rest of us we knew that their Grandfathers had different feelings toward one another, we also knew that somehow those feelings were transcended right there in that room. The audience then joined in the singing and for one brief moment we understood what it means to truly be one.

How does song work? I don't know, and I don't really care, but I do know that the unseen world, the real one, consists of vibrations of the life force energy. I also know that the anxiety of mortal life is a result of our fear-oriented mind being out of harmony with the life-giving power of the Universe. When this occurs, we are playing two clashing notes on our spiritual piano. Rather than simply recognizing the problem and trying a new note, we tend to cling to our melody and demand that the universe change keys. It will never happen. The universe is always in tune. Our challenge is to use the universe as our tuning key. This doesn't mean that we must make beautiful music every step of the way, but that we learn to recognize when we are in tune, and use this as our guide until we resonate as the universe, and truly become one.

What does this have to do with singing a song? When we sing a song, our mind is distracted. It is difficult for your mind to dwell on the impending fears of the day and sing a song at the same time. You can probably do it, but if you keep on singing it will take too much energy to do both, and your fears will eventually dissipate.

Singing is also a powerful way to implant messages into your subconscious mind, so pick songs that say the kind of thing you want to hear. You can even make up your own song with custom verses made especially for you. Make them funny, or interesting, or applicable, and sing them over and over. It cannot help but make you feel better.

Another value in singing is that there is no purpose in it. You aren't singing to improve cash flow or to get a better job or a better mate, you're just singing for the joy of it. That is the way the universe would like us to live our life — for the pure joy of it. If you want to really experience an analogy of the eternities try singing in a choir. There is something about working together to create harmony that transcends the mortal experience. It is a taste of our deific mission. It is the eternities coming to life. It is residing in our celestial home until the final bar has been sung. It is the joy of creating harmony with our fellow man that brings the dream to life.

Singing will definitely help even if you hum quietly at your desk, but if you want mass effect, then belt it out. You may not think this is appropriate because no one else would get their work done or because you are the timid type who just doesn't do that sort of thing. If that's the case belt it out in your car — the perfect isolated portable acoustic sound chamber. Who cares what your fellow commuters think. Just smile back at them — maybe you'll teach them a thing or two.

A few weeks ago I went skiing for the first time in a couple of years with a friend named Bill. After a couple of runs is was clear that I just wasn't getting it. We stopped at the top of a precipice and he asked me "What is your song today?" I had completely forgotten that one of the most important elements of good skiing is to have the right song in your head. I confessed that I didn't have one. He told me that he was using "Miss America" and he thought I might like to try it. I did, it didn't work, neither did "Wang Chung" or "Itsy Bitsy Teeny Weeny Yellow Polka Dot Bikini." Finally I tried Madonna's "True Blue" and I was hot. I don't know what happened, but I do know that just by playing this tune in my head my skiing improved 500 percent instantly. I don't care what happened either, I just know that I'm going to keep on doing anything that works that well.

All this is just a bunch of words unless it works for you — so try it. Wherever you are, whatever you are doing, however you feel, sing a song. Right now. Don't worry about singing the right song or knowing the words, or even having words. Make up the song if you want to. It can even be a one-note chant. Take a deep breath and — OOOOOOOOOOOOOhm. You may not know it yet, but you are already starting to feel better. Just keep it up for a while and sure enough you will notice a significant difference in the way you feel. Your problems will seem more manageable, your blessings will seem more abundant, and you will bring a sense of peace to everything you do.

I think ABBA says it best in the song, *I Have a Dream.*

> *I have a dream,*
> *A song to sing.*
> *That helps me through,*
> *Reality.*

20

Get Started

I f you want to feel better, start doing something. Not just anything, but something that is clearly on the path to where you dream of being. If you dream of having your own business, take a class or read a book on business. If you dream of being a pilot, buy the text book or go to an air show. If you would like your bathroom remodeled, go in there right now and rip the moldings off the wall or tear the wallpaper to pieces. If you dream of being a writer, go get a notebook and a pen and start writing — right now.

One of the main reasons we limit our feelings of joy is because we don't do the things we really like to do. The main reason we don't do the things we want to do is fear of the unknown. This is easy to understand if our dream is to be a test pilot or a professional bungy-cord jumper, but it is the same fear that keeps us from embarking on our journey whether it be starting a club, going to school, or remodeling the bathroom. "Will I succeed? What color will I choose? What if it looks worse when I'm done? What if I run out of money. What if everyone hates it? What if I can't hang wallpaper. What if I have to move some pipes? What if I end up with the ugliest bathroom in the trailer court? Oh my God, what would people think?"

On and on go the doubts and fears, and they'll never stop until you stop them. The best way to stop them is to get going — go in right now and rip the wallpaper off. Then you won't have any choice.

You see, the thing that holds you up does not exist. It is only your self-imposed fear of the future that is stopping you. The truth is that the future doesn't exist and it never will. The problem is that we look at this monolithic task and ask ourselves, "Can I do this?" rather than asking, "What is my next step?" When you ask yourself "Can I do this?" the answer is sure to be "No", or "maybe," at best. If you already knew you could do it, you would have already done it. When you look at the whole project you see that you don't know how to wallpaper, you hate to paint, you don't know the slightest thing about plumbing, and you'll have to buy a saw, and who knows how much money this will cost. Suddenly your bathroom has turned into a slave labor camp from which you may never escape.

There is more value in just starting than you think. For one, you see yourself taking a tangible step, however small, in the direction you would like to go. This alone will make you feel better. Even more beneficial is the message you are sending to the universe. You are voting for yourself; you are saying, "I can do this." You are letting the cosmic powers of your being know what it is you want to do.

"Whatever you can do, or dream you can, begin it.

Boldness has genius, power and magic in it." What Goethe is telling us is that we can always take the next step. We can learn how to cut molding, we can call a plumber, we can save pop cans until we can afford a saw, we can figure out how to paint, and everyone but me can hang wallpaper. Whatever it is we are striving for, we can always take the next step. The secret is that the second step will not be revealed until we take the first one. This is one of the mysteries of life that is holding many of us back. We act like an infant who does not climb up the first step because he cannot see how he is going to get up the fifth one.

"In God we trust," "I cast my burdens upon the Lord," "I move forward in faith," "Yea though I walk through the valley of death I fear no . . ." hollow words, a mute testimony to a society that has learned to stand at the bottom of the stairs and mourn. It is only when we begin to move that grace can have a place in our lives. We sit at the bottom of the stairs weeping because we have been dealt an unfair hand. When you see with your mortal eyes the red carpet laid out in every direction, your perspective becomes considerably different. You will watch the miracles of the Universe unfold in your life in ways you had never dreamed possible. Once you start on this path of unfolding, you will discover that the rapid progress you are making is a miniscule blessing compared with the love you will feel. You will watch the unseen hand paving a way before you. You will see the bridge appear every time you step into the chasm. Before long you will come to know deep within your being that there is, and always has been, an unseen power guiding your every step. This knowing will fill you with wonder, peace, confidence, and with the feeling of being part of something so much greater than yourself.

The other day I was flipping through a fake book when I came to the song *Blue Moon.* I really liked the words so the next week I asked my piano teacher, Gay, if she would play it for me. She immediately went into this extraordinary rendition which I recognized immediately and got excited about learning to play — until I looked at the music. Gay sensed my hesitation and encouraged me saying I could be playing it in a couple of weeks. There were so many notes and flats and sharps and squiggly things I was sure it would take me a couple of years at best. I wanted to play it anyway so I went home and figured out the first measure, and the second, and played them each a few dozen times. Then I noticed that these measures were repeated several times throughout the song. Maybe there was hope. Sure enough, two weeks later I could belt out a pretty good sounding rendition of *Blue Moon.* Looking back I see that 99 percent of the obstacles were in my mind, and that as soon as I got started, the obstacles fell by the wayside until I arrived at the place I wanted to be.

Grace is kind of like riding a bicycle. It seems impossible if you're not moving, and dangerous if you move. You think you can do it once you get going — but you can't get going until you do it. Let's go have another beer. We sit in the pub contemplating our dilemma when out the window we see it with our own eyes. A little girl riding a bicycle with "no hands." Is it possible, how can she do that? I would love to be able to do that.

You start to complain about the lousy hand you have been dealt when you see the band-aids on her elbows and her skinned up knees. She doesn't even notice them anymore, but you do.

You get up to leave, "Where are you going?" ask your fellow commiserators.

"To get a bike" you respond."

"Why are you going to get a bike if you can't ride one?" they ask.

"I don't exactly know, but I don't think I'm ever going to learn to ride one if I don't get one first."

What is your dream? Where do you want to be? What would you enjoy? What is your life about? What would you like to be doing right now? If you could do anything you want for a living, what would it be? Answer one of these questions and get started — right now! You will immediately feel better, you will begin to develop an internal sense of empowerment, and you will begin to look forward to a brighter tomorrow even though we both know that it doesn't really exist.

"Breathe the breath of life,
And be free."

21

The Breath Of Life

*T*he breath of life, prana, the breath of God, the balm of breath, whatever you want to call it, is a powerful spiritual regenerator. It is the source of your mortal life, it is a major regenerating factor in your body, it is the creative force of the universe, yet it is almost completely ignored by our intellectual society.

Your parents waited anxiously for the glorious moment when you took your first breath. All present wept with joy as the spirit of life filled your minute body and you began your sojourn on this earth. But within minutes, or seconds, this glorious gift of breath was forgotten. You put it on automatic and haven't thought about it since. Yet through some power beyond our comprehension, nature has provided a way for our body to accept this gift of life and keep it flowing through our being until our final mortal moment, often called our "Last breath," when the pool of prana we call "me" departs our mortal vehicle and returns to universal breath. Funny how we take for granted what we don't have to struggle for, and we struggle for what we don't need at all.

Breathing is not merely a mechanical function like blinking your eyes or bending your knee, it is the flow of the life force through your being. Breath is the connection between your conscious mind and your unconscious mind. It is the only essential function of your body you have a choice to operate consciously, or ignore completely. In addition to keeping you alive, your breath also:

- Circulates your lymphatic system
- Nourishes the pool of life force within you
- Provides an exchange and renewal of your cells
- Connects your conscious mind to your unconscious mind
- Connects your body to your consciousness
- Provides a vehicle for consciousness control

If air had color we would think of the entire breathing process differently, but as usual, we don't think there is power in anything we cannot see. So we go on living an unconscious life. Thinking polluted thoughts, breathing polluted air, eating polluted food and living a polluted life. It may be fun, it may give you status or pleasure or cheap thrills, but it never gets you what you really want. What you really want is love, and to know that you are a totally loved and absolutely essential part of the universe.

In the 1940s Dr. Lamaze realized that a woman in labor could virtually eliminate the pain of childbirth by controlling her focus and her breath. Incredible, I wouldn't have believed it had I not watched it work, four times. In the midst of what was obviously intense pain, my darling wife began her breathing and sure enough, I could see the pain subside. It didn't make the job any easier, but at least it wasn't as painful.

I once hit myself in the shin with an axe and, while I was writhing on the ground in pain, my wife suggested that I breathe. At first I thought she was joking, but she began coaching me as if I were in labor. In desperation I started "stage three breathing" to humor her. Within minutes my pain had subsided and I was able to relax. Once again I experienced first hand the incredible power of breath.

Some of you are undoubtedly thinking that this is impossible, that breathing is nothing more than a biological function that provides our body with the molecular structures necessary to sustain life. While that is true, when we recognize that life is only an analogy of reality, we will also recognize that the counterpart of the molecular structures that sustain mortal life is the ever-flowing life force of the universe that sustains our inner being. It is the ocean of life ebbing and flowing on the shores of our immortal soul.

I know at this point many dyed-in-the-wool, letter-of-the-law dogmatists may have some doubts. If you have any doubts that this is true I challenge you to experience a Prana rebirthing experience. No excuses. The process consists only of controlling your breathing. Incredible as it may sound, through the process of controlling our breath we can experience the infinite. We can transcend the mortal world. We can go to the "Place" the Holy men have been describing to us for millennia. We can become "Quickened and see God." This is not some abstract feeling that you might feel or you might not. It is a knowing, a going beyond, a transcending, a near-death experience without the near-death part. It is an increase of consciousness to the point where you become truth. A point where you can see clearly that you are an infinite, unbounded child of the ages — totally and completely loved, and absolutely essential to the universe. You who once questioned your own self-worth, now see yourself as an essential piece of the cosmic puzzle.

What can you do right now? Breathe deeply — right now. Three deep breaths, slowly and as deeply as you can. Ready; 1. Breathe in — exhale 2. Breathe in — exhale 3. Breathe in — exhale. It worked. You may feel noticeably better, or the change may be so small or you may be so out of tune that you hardly notice it at all, but it worked. You feel a little bit better. When you increase the flow of life force through your being, your consciousness rises and you feel better. It cannot be otherwise.

So the next time you are bothered, your job is the pits, your wife is a crab, or some dogma is driving you crazy, take a moment to breath. In, out, in, out, keep on going, give yourself five minutes to breath deeply with your focus on the breathing. For five minutes leave your precious problems behind and become totally aware of your breath. If you do this, and truly focus on your breath there will come a time when you will weep in gratitude for the gift of another breath. A gift without which your party will be over, a gift for which the kings of the ages would gladly trade their entire kingdom. A breath so precious that we will gladly trade everything we think we own for just one more. All this we give for one more breath, yet we take for granted the thousands that are given to us each day.

Acknowledge the gift, embrace it, let it into your life. No matter what else is going on in your world, you will feel a little bit better right now. What more could you ask of life? You will know that regardless of who you are, or what you think, or what you've done, you are an integral part of this universe, and you are loved totally and completely by a power so immense and so loving that it is beyond your mortal comprehension. Once you feel it, and know it to be true, your life will never be the same again.

*"Nothing is either good or bad
But thinking makes it so."*
                                        Shakespeare

22

Share Your Secret

Quietly, to yourself, think of the one thing you most want no one to know about you. Maybe you had an affair, or a nose job; maybe you stole something once, cheated on your income taxes or had an abortion. Sometimes the dirty deed seems absurd. I had a woman confess to me in tears that years ago she had given away the family dog when they were moving, and she had told her kids it had run away. I could literally see the burden lift from her as she shared the experience with me. She then proceeded to tell her now adult children what she had done and they readily forgave her. When I saw her next she was a different person. She knew that she was loved and accepted regardless of what she had done. Something she hadn't known before.

Your secret could be as trivial as not wanting people to know that your car is leased or that you owe people money. Maybe it is that you wish you were skinny, that you got your dress at Goodwill, or that you skipped church once back in 1972. Whatever it is, take a moment to think of the one thing you most want to keep secret. Okay, got it? The one thing you want no one to know. Make sure your clear about this and complete this sentence to yourself.

"The one thing I don't want anyone to know about me is that:

_____."

Now for step #2, go tell someone.

"Arruuuggghhh. No way am I going to tell anyone that" is the usual response. That's why you haven't, but if you knew how much better you'd feel right now, and for the rest of your life, you'd run out and shout it from the roof top.

Although it doesn't really matter who you tell, it might be helpful to pick an appropriate person. It may not be effective to tell your Catholic mother-in-law that you cheated on her daughter, and you may not want to tell the parish loud mouth that you lust after the preacher's wife. The important thing is that you do it. Think of the worst thing you have ever done and find someone you can tell. Pick someone who won't fly off the handle and scream at you about the irresponsible louse you are. If you're a church goer, your preacher might do, or maybe the preacher of a different church, or maybe the preacher of a different church in a different city — or country.

You might want to dress in your worst clothes and go downtown with a bottle in a bag. Sit in a dirty alley and strike up a conversation with the first wino that comes along. Listen to his woes and his philosophy for a while, and then unload on him. Compared to what you've just heard you probably won't have much trouble telling him that you stole lunch money in 3rd grade or that you think your mother's a creep. Go easy on him though. He'll probably laugh you out of the alley if he thinks this is your big life secret you're sharing with him. I know this sounds absurd, but not only will you feel better, you'll probably learn something too.

Contrary to popular belief, the wino may serve you every bit as well as the preacher. You may also find that he has some of the most practical counsel you've ever heard. The preacher does not have any God-given right to forgive you, but you will think he does because you will truly feel better when you tell him your secret. The reason preachers sometimes work better is because we believe they represent God. Once we understand that we all represent God, the title of the person we choose to confide in becomes moot. Besides, you might be doing the wino a favor, he probably doesn't get as many opportunities to relieve burdens as the preacher does.

I once spoke with one man who felt that he was living in the depths of sin because he found women other than his wife attractive. I told him that I too found women other than his wife attractive. What does he think? That we're supposed to go through life until we find the most attractive woman in the world, marry her, and have our optical brain synapses altered so that we live in the delusion that we, and we alone, have married Aphrodite? What else could explain his absurd belief?

Our secrets may seem ridiculous to others, yet to us they are our reality and they seem so real, and so ominous, and so bad that we would rather give up our life than have the truth be known.

Where do we get these absurd beliefs? Probably

from well-meaning "experts" called parents, teachers, clergy and other "big people." They may not have even said it, but it was our interpretation, and at the time we probably believed they were speaking for God, or that they were God. But now that we're "grown up," it's time to dump these burdens.

The mechanics of it is that "we are our secrets." We become what we hold inside. If we broadcast the treasure and keep the trash, we become the trash. If we keep the treasure to ourselves and reveal our trash, we become the treasure. This doesn't mean you have to spread your dirty laundry all over town, it just means that you have to unload your extra baggage on someone else. Don't worry about them, they'll throw the trash away immediately, like you would have done years ago if you had only known how.

These secrets are a burden that you need not carry around. Not because they are bad or because it's a sin, but because it takes effort to conceal truth, and this effort drains you every minute — it zaps the life-giving force right out of your being. This will not be an easy step, but it is likely to be one of the most rapid and effective steps you can take into the world of peace that awaits you. So do it anyway.

If you promise to tell your secret I'll tell you one of mine. Okay. Ready? You've thought of yours, now here is one of mine. I am scared to publish this book. That may not seem like much to you, but to me it is a real fear, and I don't want anyone to know it, but I do feel much better knowing that you know that no matter how successful or unsuccessful this book is, I am a real person with real fears, and that publishing it is facing one of my fears and taking one small step toward my divine destiny. Now, tell me, what is your secret?

23

Tell The Truth

*T*he common belief is that the harm in telling a lie, or an untruth, lays in the deception which you imposed on the person to whom you lied. I used to believe that too, but now that I see a little more clearly, I have a difficult time getting back to a place where that makes sense. The burden of a lie is imposed upon the liar and the liar alone. There may be others who chose to let the lie upset them, that is their challenge. The only one who has no choice other than to be burdened by a lie is the one who told it, and the only ransom that can be paid to free the liar from the prison of deceit, is truth.

What is the purpose of a lie? To attempt to get people to deal with you on some basis other than the truth. You have the misguided notion that you will get more of something you want by deceit. The problem is that you get this little dribble of whatever it is you want that lasts a few seconds, and you now have a lie which you must support — forever.

On and on we go adding burden after burden to our emotional backpack until we become so burdened we can hardly stand up. There are only two ways out, tell the truth, or die. The problem is that when we die the truth will be known anyway so why not ransom your life with the truth right now and spend the remaining years of your life living?

On one occasion I drove one of my work trucks to a nice restaurant to meet my family for dinner. When I arrived there was no place to park. I circled the parking lot several times and was rather annoyed at some inconsiderate SOB who had parked his Mercedes in two slots to avoid getting scratched. I circled the lot a few more times and then figured I could park in one of the slots next to the Mercedes if I let the side of my truck push up against the bushes.

Halfway through dinner we were asked by the maitre d' if anyone at our table had a silver pickup truck. I acknowledged that it was mine and I walked out to the parking lot with an irate Mercedes driver (who wasn't willing to climb into the passenger's side of his car) and his female fixture.

"How could you? I can't believe you would park your truck so close to my Mercedes. Who do you think you are?"

On and on he raved about how inconsiderate I was and how important his car was and how unimportant my truck was, and why I would drive a truck to a restaurant like this. When we were almost to his car I stopped.

"This really bothers you, doesn't it?"

"Of course it bothers me!" he screamed. "It should

bother you too, but you obviously don't care if someone bangs their door into your truck. Do you know how much it costs to paint a car like this?"

"No."

"A bunch, I'll tell you that much, and when I own something I take care of it. I don't go around letting punk kids scratch it all up with their junker trucks."

"Excuse me for saying so, but in the first place I didn't touch your car, in the second place, it appears to me that your car owns you, and in the third place, I don't think you should buy a car like this if you can't afford to take care of it." I moved my truck while this poor soul screamed at me some more, loaded his female fixture into the passenger's seat and squealed his tires halfway across town.

What does this have to do with telling the truth? A lot. We think of lies as verbal utterances that are inconsistent with our beliefs. The truth is that anytime we represent ourselves as something other than what we are — it's a lie, and we alone pay the price.

Mr. Mercedes was not upset because his paint might get chipped or because he might have to climb into his car from the passenger side. He was upset because he was caught in his lie. His lie was that he felt he was important or that he was rich or that he felt powerful, or that he was master of every situation. Whatever it was, it is taking its toll on his life. His lie also had nothing to do with his car. There is nothing inherently wrong or destructive about parking in two spots or having a Mercedes, or a Rolls-Royce, or a private jet or your own country. The problem lies in your emotional attachment to these things. If you are using these contrivances to represent yourself as something other than what you are, therein lies the problem.

It is the discrepancy between what we are and what

we say we are that wreaks the havoc in our lives. Why not start bringing these two closer together right now. How? The easiest way is to tell the truth, to totally and completely stop lying. This sounds easy because none of us think of ourselves as liars. The truth is that none of us are liars, but all of us attempt to deceive one another in various subtle ways at one time or another, often without even knowing it.

This doesn't mean that you have to be brutally honest. When your grandmother asks what you think of her dog-ugly new coat you don't have to say "Gee grandma, I think that's the dog-ugliest coat I've ever seen." You say "Gee Grandma, that coat goes beautifully with your hair," or "That's really going to keep you warm this winter." or "You look good Grandma, but why don't you try this yellow one on. I think it will look even better."

Why do we lie? We lie because we are insecure. No exceptions. Every lie, every deceit, every misrepresentation is a result of a feeling of inadequacy on our part. They are an effort to avoid pain or to bring about pleasure that we believe we could not have if the truth were known.

Actually lies are a great way to avoid pain and a great way to avoid the negative consequences of your actions. They're fast, easy, cheap, and no one will ever know the difference. The only drawback is that you will always know the difference. A lie adds to the burden you are carrying, and unless you do something about it you will carry it to your grave.

The trick to becoming a Master is to experience your word as law. First with the little things; the size of your shoes, your age, or the length of the fish you caught, and then gradually expanding into commands of the universe. Tree, grow. Mountain, move. Child be healed. The universe eagerly awaits the command of a congruent man.

But who would obey one who cannot be true to himself?

When you are at the place of total truth you can tell anyone anything at any time. You have nothing to hide, no secrets, no burdens; you don't have to figure out what to say, you simply tell the truth. It is the easiest way to live. Life becomes an effortless joy, a graceful moving from one peaceful moment to the next, rather than a frantic effort to conceal deceit. Deceit which is billowing forth with our every breath. Deceit which becomes a part of our very being until we call upon the truth to free us — that we may become who it is we are here to become.

Nothing is more pleasing than a person who is real. A person who admits that he is tired or broke or old or ugly; a person who writes three and one half hours on his time card and you know you got a good deal; a person who you can talk and laugh and live in peace with because he isn't trying to hide anything or be anything, and he isn't trying to live up to anyone's expectations except his own. A person whose 14 inch fish you know will measure out to over 14 inches. There is only one person you are going to be spending the eternities with. What kind of person do you want that to be?

Most lies are not verbal. They are symbolic. They take the form of contraptions we hide behind to solicit acclaim for our wealth, or cosmetics we hide behind to solicit acclaim for our beauty; or "friends" we collect to support our insecurities about our social acceptance. Sometimes they escape as alterations of our dress size or denial of our past. Other times they appear as undue tolerance of another at the expense of our emotional well-being, or alterations in our accountability. Make no mistake, whatever the form, you are accountable. Your life's mission is to get your mortal life to conform to your spiritual life. In other words, to express what you really are. It is only when we are expressing our truth that we can move ahead. You can lie all day long; you may deceive the world, but you will never deceive yourself, and in the final analysis that is all that really matters.

24

"Thank You"

*"You ain't gettin' nothin'
'till you're glad for what you got."*

"T hank somebody, what good can that do? Besides, what has anyone done to deserve being thanked?" It has nothing to do with their deserving to be thanked. It has only to do with your desire to thank them. If you don't believe me try thanking those people in your life who least deserve it. The next time your business associates drag their feet forever to get something done, thank them for doing it. Let them know in a sincere way that you really appreciate them and what they've done. They may think you're crazy, but you will feel better, and they will work a lot more efficiently in the future. The opportunities are endless — the gas station attendant, the grocery store clerk, your doctor. Or even better, how about your spouse, your kids, your parents, or your neighbor. You know, all the people you take for granted.

If you really want to feel good make your thanks sincere. Watch the grocery clerk pack your bags and realize that she is putting out effort for you. Recognize her as another human being who has challenges and dreams all her own. Wonder what lies ahead for her in her life. Wish the best for her; look her in the eye and say, "Thank You." If you really want to feel better use her name if you know it. People really respond when you use their name, and you'll feel better right now!

There are a zillion other ways to say thank you besides saying it. There are the traditional ways like sending flowers or a thank you note, and there are the incident specific ways that only you know about. Yesterday my wife was feeling pressured because the phone kept ringing, soccer was at the same time as ballet, our horses were on the neighbor's lawn, we're having guests over, the house was a mess and somebody missed the school bus. She arrived home with all four kids about 6:30 at night to find a plate full of peanut butter and jelly sandwiches and drinks on the table. She felt so loved and appreciated she had tears in her eyes. Not because she likes peanut butter and jelly sandwiches, but because I had thanked her in a way that nobody else would have understood. What makes this even more significant is that this was the first time I have ever made a complete meal for our family that they would eat. Anyway, it took me about 15 minutes; I'll be reminding her about it for years to come, and I feel better right now. Next time you have the chance to thank someone, don't waste it with a quick "Thanks-Fred-see-you-later." Take the time to shake Fred's hand, look him in the eye and say "Fred, I want to thank you for helping out at school today. I don't know how I would have handled all the little buggers if you weren't there." Chances are Fred will discount his value and pass off his contribution — don't let him. Even if he does, it doesn't matter because you will feel better anyway.

There are two ways to motivate people. With candy, or with a whip. The whip only works temporarily and makes things worse for the next time. The candy works forever, and one of the best-tasting candies in the world is being appreciated. Believe it or not, most of the things people do are in an effort to be appreciated or admired by others. Knowing this gives us a powerful behavior modification tool to use. A tool we carry with us all the time which makes us feel better every time we use it. It is our ability to express our appreciation. Try it out on those around you. I am certain that if you would simply ignore all the negative behavior that went on around you, and express your appreciation for all the positive behavior, no matter how little of it there is, you would very shortly extinguish the negative, and the positive would become a way of life. This may sound too simple, but I don't think there is anything you could do to change your life and the lives of those around you as effectively as following this simple, free, easily implementable plan.

Don't forget to thank your kids. Sometimes we start to think of our children as little mess-up-the-house machines that make noise, cost money, and take up all of our time. We forget that they are living, loving children of the Universe who are doing the best they know how, and who deserve our utmost respect. You have no idea how much it means to them to know that they are deeply appreciated by their parents. If they all knew they were appreciated by their parents, the problems with the youth of the world would disappear overnight.

This is where I get my greatest joy. I sneak into my children's rooms at night, put my arm around them and say "Bradley, I appreciate the way you helped Jonathan at soccer practice today," or "Jessica, thank you for the note you wrote on my calendar," or "Jonathan, I appreciate the way you help take care of Ryan." Then a funny thing happens, the little rascals look up into my eyes with such pride, such love and admiration, as if they had just been complimented by God. I look into their little eyes and see a vibrant spirit who loves me unconditionally, who lives in awe and respect of me in spite of my imperfections, and I am overwhelmed by an intense feeling of love. A powerful taste of the joy we can experience if we will only allow ourselves to be grateful for the untold blessing of life. Then I kneel down, tuck them in, kiss their little noses, and say a few "thank yous" of my own.

25

Your Life Story

The Sages of the Ages have been telling us to write it down for millennia untold. Our holy books are the legacy of those who did, our libraries are full of autobiographies, we buy our kids a baby journal, but we never record our own story. If our life is worth living it is worth recording.

Some of you may be wondering whether your life is indeed worth living. It goes like this; "I haven't saved anyone's life, invented anything, cured a disease or written a book; I've never even reached one of my goals or done anything that matters. As a matter of fact, I really haven't done anything except eat and sleep and drink beer. Come to think of it, my life has been one big torment. I think I was happy once, as a kid maybe, but now? I haven't done anything worth writing down in years, decades maybe." Therein lies the first fallacy.

Fallacy #1: "In order for your life story to be worth recording it must be one of great importance."

"... and then the little girl picked a flower and gave it to her mother, and her mother loved her and they had a perfect life and nothing ever went wrong because they lived in Happyland, and nothing ever went wrong in Happyland.

Then one day the little girl grew up and married the wonderful boy next door and her parents loved him too and they had ten children through immaculate conception and they were all healthy, all the time and his parents gave them $100,000 each year so they could go to college and hire good help because they wanted their grandchildren to be happy. Then, when he graduated, he got the first job he applied for and within a week they promoted him to be the President of the company and gave him a big raise. He then decided that he would only work 10 or 20 hours a week and take weekdays off so he could spend time with his family. And they lived happily ever after in a state of total bliss."

Yawn — snore — boooorrrring. What a dull story. It was probably all you could do to get through one paragraph of that stuff, yet that is the stuff we think we should write, right? Wrong. Whether you are writing for yourselves or your progenitors, you've got to write the stuff of life. What is going on in your mind? What challenges are you facing? How do you think you might overcome them? How committed are you? How does it turn out? How do you feel?

"... today was a better day than most because nothing disastrous happened, but I still struggle. I hate struggle. I guess I'm scared. I quit my job to start this business and it's not going quite as well as I had hoped, and I don't know what I'm going to do. I've tried everything I can think of, but I don't seem to be able to make enough money, especially with our increased medical expenses. Sometimes I resent my wife for getting sick, I know it's not her fault, but it's pulling us under.

"This would be easy if I were single, I could live in my truck and eat berries for a few months until I got things going. But then, I probably wouldn't have quit if it wasn't for my family because I was making enough to be comfortable by myself. Who knows? I think I did this for my family, but I always wanted to go into business for myself. Who cares, it's done and look at what's happening. But I didn't really have any other choice. My job was going nowhere, no money, no retirement, no bonuses, no nothing except work 'till you die.

"Maybe this will work out, I don't know. I'm going to go see Mr. McDaniel tomorrow, maybe he'll carry my stuff in his store. That would be great, that would probably take care of everything. Gotta go, wish me luck. Good luck."

No earth-shattering news, no flowers, no lace, and no golden fleece. Just a man alone with his thoughts. Yet, it's much more interesting than Happyland. Don't you want to help the guy, or go tell Mr. McDaniel how good his stuff is. I want to know what happened. Wouldn't it be comforting for a struggling entrepreneur with a young family to read this in the journal of the man who one day ended up owning an international chain of McDaniel's stores.

No matter how your life is unfolding, you will find that your story, written from the heart, will always be of great interest. If you don't believe me, try it for a few months and then go back and see what you've written.

Remember, the greatest value in the story is to the writer, so don't worry about doing it right or proper or making it interesting, just write what you feel. This brings us to fallacy #2.

Fallacy #2; "You are recording your life for the benefit of others"

Although others will undoubtedly benefit from reading your journal, the reason the Sages advocate the keeping of a journal is not so that your great-grandkids will have something to read, but because it is good therapy. It is probably one of the most effective forms of self-therapy you can conduct. For those of you who don't think you need therapy we'll call it by a different name — like more joy, or burden relief, or greater peace. Whatever you want to call it, we all need it. That's why we're all knocking around down here.

Like our body, our mind and spirit will repair themselves if given the chance. The problem is we keep goring the wound, over and over, every moment of every day, proving to ourselves that what we believe is true.

When our thoughts and feelings are whirring around in our biocomputer, we can't get them to stop long enough to take a look at them and see if they are serving us. However, if we will write down our thoughts and feelings, we have in effect taken a snapshot of the weapons we are using to irritate our psychic wounds. We don't have to be a cosmic psychologist or a rabbi par excellent for this to work. All we have to do is do it. Our mind will take care of the rest. We don't even have to know that change is taking place. As a matter of fact, it is probably better that we don't know because otherwise our devious mind would probably get in there and bungle things up.

It is easy to give other people advice, but we are rarely aware of our own faults let alone able to prescribe treatment. This is a good chance to get outside of yourself, get an objective perspective, and receive the love, compassion, and understanding of he who must be your best friend — You.

One of my greatest insights about life came as a result of keeping a journal. After jotting down a few lines about how good I felt and what was going on and some trivia of the day, I flipped back to the previous day for some reason, and read about how much pressure I felt, and how hopeless everything seemed, and how burdens were being piled upon me faster than I could possibly deal with them.

Whoever wrote that stuff obviously had a pretty rough life, and there truly wasn't much hope for him. Yet here I am the next day, same person, same challenges, same family, same clothes, same home, same car, same bills, same everything and I feel great. At that moment I came to the profound knowing that any discomfort or suffering we are experiencing is truly a result of our thinking rather than a result of circumstances. I had read this kind of stuff before, but I didn't really get it. Now I know it. It is a part of me. I know beyond a shadow of a doubt that the challenges of man lay within and I no longer waste my energy jousting with life to capture joy. (All right, I do still joust with life to give me joy, but I don't do it as often.) Anyway, that knowing alone was worth all the journal writing I'll ever do.

Now don't go out and buy a dozen notebooks that you intend to fill with five pages of memoirs every day. You know where those radical change commitments will get you. Start by committing to write a sentence every day, or a page every Sunday. Go easy on yourself, you deserve it. And remember, this is not a list of the events of the day, but a recording of your reflections at the time. How do you feel? What are your challenges? Why do you feel that way? What are you going to do about it? The deeper you get into your feelings, the more interesting will be your writing, and the more peace it will bring you.

As you get into your inner being, the place where your dreams and aspirations come from, the place where we read about the real you that transcends time and space, you will begin to notice changes in the world around you. Actually the world may not have changed at all, but you have moved to a different place and have a new perspective. You now get about as bothered by a real life disaster as you do by a movie disaster. From the distance you see that neither one is real. You are at peace about most everything. You see people as they really are, and time begins to slow down. This may seem impossible, but the quickening spoken of in all the holy books is taking place, and the role of time in your mortal life is becoming less and less apparent. Keep it up — 25 hours a day, 30, then 40 or 50. It may seem strange at first, but go with it anyway. You will soon understand that time is a contrivance of man, and that it doesn't really exist. You will see yourself as an actor on a stage of an unwritten play which you yourself are directing. You will sit back and watch the production unfold from a peaceful place in the audience, knowing that whatever happens is all right, no matter how it may seem to be at the time. You become the playwright, the director and the audience, of a never-ending drama. A drama that can drag you through the depths of hell or raise you to the pinnacle of perfection. The choice is up to you.

Conclusion

s we discussed in the beginning, the reason for everything we do is to make us feel better. Sometimes the results we get are not what we hoped for, but that was our initial purpose. If you have made some choices that haven't brought you closer to your bliss, don't berate yourself or curse your lot in life, just think of them as lessons you have learned that are bringing you ever closer to your divine destiny, and move on.

If you chose to use the methods discussed in this book be careful not to overload yourself. Just pick an area or two you would like to focus on, work on them until they are mastered, and then move on to another. So often our life-seeking strategies backfire because we try to eat the whole coconut in one bite.

You might want to start sleeping on the other side of the bed and calling people by name, or you might choose to walk around the block every day or to plant a garden. Whatever you choose, make sure it is simple and peaceful and that you don't over-commit yourself. You may not wake up tomorrow healed from a life of manic depression, but wherever you are right now, if you do any of these things you will wake up tomorrow to a sun that shines a little brighter, a world that brings you a little more joy, and an increased feeling of hope and self-acceptance deep within your being. What more can you ask for?

It is my hope that each of us will continue to make life-giving choices until we truly become one, until we experience the "peace that surpasseth all understanding" as a universal family; that we may all start feeling even better — right now!

I Am I

I am I, and thou art thee,
        That is what appears to be.
But I am thee, and thou art I,
        Though never to the mortal eye.

Were I not thee and thou not I,
        Thy pain could never make me cry.
But linked together as we be,
        We now can set each other free.

For loving you is loving me,
        And love is what we long to be.
So love yourself in every form,
        The man, the girl, the child unborn.

And know that is the only way,
        For freedom's song to come and stay.
And well up in your aching heart,
        A peace you know will never part.

Bill Chandler

Order Form

25
THINGS
YOU CAN DO TO
FEEL BETTER
RIGHT NOW!

Please send _____ copies at $10.95 each book, plus $2 shipping and handling for the first book, $1 for each additional book on the same order.

Name: _____

Address: _____

City/State/Zip:_____

Phone: Bus.: _____ Home: _____

If paying with credit card, please complete information below:

[ ] Visa [ ] MasterCard #_____

_____/_____ _____
Expiration Date   Your Signature

Please return this information with check or money order payable to:

Andante Publishing
Post Office Box 507
Redmond, Washington 98073-0507
TO ORDER TODAY CALL
800-773-3770